A PRIME MINISTER TO REMEMBER

A PRIME MINISTER TO REMEMBER

Memories of a Military Chief

ADMIRAL SUSHIL KUMAR
Former Chief of Naval Staff (1998-2001)

KONARK

Konark Publishers Pvt Ltd
New Delhi • Seattle

Konark Publishers Pvt. Ltd
206, First Floor,
Peacock Lane, Shahpur Jat,
New Delhi - 110 049
Phone: +91-11-41055065
Mob: +91 93552 93900, +91 93552 94900
e-mail: india@konarkpublishers.com
website: www.konarkpublishers.com

Konark Publishers International
8615, 13th Ave SW,
Seattle, WA 98106
Phone: (415) 409-9988
e-mail: us@konarkpublishers.com

Cataloging in Publication Data--DK
Courtesy: D.K. Agencies (P) Ltd. <docinfo@dkagencies.com>

Kumar, Sushil (Admiral), author.
A prime minister to remember : memories of a military chief / Admiral Sushil Kumar.
pages cm
ISBN 9789322008963

1. Kumar, Sushil (Admiral) 2. Admirals--India--Biography.
3. India--History, Naval. 4. Vajpayee, Atal Bihari, 1924-2018. I. Title.

LCC V64.I42K86 2019 | DDC 359.4092 23

Edited by Dipali Singh
Book design by Misha Oberoi
Typeset by 3P Solutions, New Delhi
Printed and bound at Thomson Press (India) Ltd.

It is to my wife Venita Kumar and daughter
Anishya Kumar that I dedicate this book, for it was they who
motivated me to document my memories of the
late Atal Bihari Vajpayee when he was the Prime Minister
and I happened to serve as an armed forces' Chief.

CONTENTS

Anchoring an Idea ix
Publisher's Note xi
Preface xiii
Acknowledgements xix

PART 1: THE VAJPAYEE YEARS 1
1. The Spring of 1999: Kargil Begins 3
2. A Lesson from Kargil: Integrating the Three Services 12
3. Bridging the Gap in Civil–Military Relations 22
4. First International Fleet Review: Bridges of Friendship 27
5. Dealing with China: The Vajpayee Way 32
6. Parliament Terror Attack and Operation Parakram 41
7. Operation Enduring Freedom 45
8. Hijacking of IC 814: A Five-day Ordeal 51
9. Attention, All Hands!: Prime Minister on Board 55
10. Operation Alondra Rainbow: Glory to the Nation 59
11. In a Lighter Vein 65

PART II: LOOKING BACK 77
12. If Wishes Were Horses 79
13. Glory at Sea: Operation Cactus 88
14. Down by the Sea: Facing the Ground Reality 94
15. Off the Chest: The Barak–Trishul Controversy 100

PART III: THE VAJPAYEE LEGACY 109
Epilogue 133

ANCHORING AN IDEA

One had heard in military circles that wives usually got jittery when their husbands' date of retirement was approaching. With nothing to do after hanging up their boots, these soulmates could turn out to be a nuisance in the house.

I suspect my wife Venita may have had the same sort of gut feeling, for she often tried to persuade (or rather, nagged!) me to write my memoirs or do something to occupy myself. Many years went by and we lived on in harmony, with not too many hiccups.

Then came the moment on 16 August 2018, when former Prime Minister Atal Bihari Vajpayee passed away. The glowing tributes paid to his statesmanship came from across the political spectrum and the accolades he received worldwide were from people belonging to all walks of life. But strangely, what had remained unsaid was the huge impact that Vajpayeeji had on the armed forces of India.

I recollected those eventful years (1998 to 2001) that I had spent as the Navy Chief when Atal Bihari Vajpayee was the Prime Minister of India. He had been very closely involved with the Indian armed forces during major operational events ranging from the Kargil war of 1999, the hijacking of IC 814, and the terror attack on the Indian Parliament in December 2001.

Quite apart from his statecraft, it was Vajpayeeji's earnest desire to understand our military ethos that enabled him to bring out the best in our fighting forces with a distinctly personal touch. That had been the hallmark of the Vajpayee era and this is what made me pen down my thoughts on what Vajpayee meant to the armed forces.

This book is an account of my impressions of our former Prime Minister Vajpayee and does not boast of being a biography. It merely reflects his unique handling of the armed forces of India as an instrument of state power and how his decisions showed his strategic understanding.

PUBLISHER'S NOTE

An explanation is needed on the methodology used to document the memories of Admiral Sushil Kumar, who served as the Chief of the Indian Navy from 1998 to 2001, when the Prime Minister was Atal Bihari Vajpayee.

The central theme of this book is the impact that Prime Minister Vajpayee had on India's armed forces, as personally experienced by the Admiral during his tenure as the Navy Chief and later as the Chairman of the Chiefs of Staff Committee.

To appreciate this perspective, the editors have dovetailed the earlier events and experiences that shaped the career of Admiral Sushil Kumar during four decades of active duty with the armed forces.

This mosaic of experiences adds authenticity to the author's first-hand account of the understanding that Prime Minister Vajpayee had of his armed forces and his rapport with the Army, Navy and Air Force Chiefs.

12 March 2019

K.P.R. Nair,
MD, Konark Publishers Pvt Ltd

PREFACE

'Being at the right place at the right time' is a cliche that I gracefully acknowledge, for I was truly fortunate to serve as the Navy Chief when Atal Bihari Vajpayee was the Prime Minister of India.

When he passed away in August 2018, glowing tributes were paid to Vajpayeeji for his unmatched political acumen. Besides that, the profuse praise for his statesmanship and sterling human qualities will surely remain etched forever in the history of independent India. But perhaps, what has remained unsaid is the impact that Prime Minister Vajpayee had on the armed forces of our country.

The military will always remember Vajpayee for his personal rapport with the armed forces of India. In his own quiet and unassuming way he had institutionalised a procedure for the Chiefs of the Army, Navy and Air Force to meet him privately at his residence. Strategy and tactics were never discussed at this weekly interaction with the Prime Minister, but he showed his earnest desire to understand his armed forces and gain their confidence. Being a man of few words, the Prime Minister hardly spoke during these meetings. Instead, we Military Chiefs did all the talking, which centred on military ethos and life in the forward areas.

This was Vajpayee's personal touch and the synergy that it infused into the rank and file of the armed forces had a multiplying effect during the Kargil war. Matching his personal touch was the Prime Minister's high-calibre, inclusive brand of political leadership, which in a manner of speaking was like a good shepherd who keeps his flock together. To a large extent this also bridged the gap in the civil–military divide that has been a chronic problem in India.

The consummate ease with which Prime Minister Vajpayee handled tricky operational situations would have given Kautilya, the ancient statesman who wrote *Arthashastra*, the famous treatise on statecraft, something to think about. One such example was during a meeting of the Cabinet Committee on Security (CCS) soon after the 9/11 terror attacks in the US. High-level delegations came to India with a special request from the US President to commit the Indian armed forces to a US-led war against Afghanistan. Opinions were sharply divided within the CCS, but the armed forces' Chiefs unanimously opposed the idea. As the American request turned into a greasy pole, Prime Minister Vajpayee graciously put the controversy to rest forever, merely by saying the issue needed more thought. What is more, the panache with which he gave his decision was a subtle lesson in how to bridge the gap in civil–military relations.

As the Navy Chief, my tenure with Prime Minister Vajpayee was during an eventful period with challenging operational events that included the Kargil war of 1999, the hijacking of the Indian Airlines IC 814 aircraft in December 1999 and the terror attack on the Parliament of India in December 2001.

It was during the Kargil war that Prime Minister Vajpayee's iron will came to the fore. He may have felt personally betrayed by Pakistan soon after his peace initiative, but he put all that behind him and galvanised our armed forces to evict the Pakistani intruders from their well-entrenched positions inside our territory along the Himalayan border. Not only was the Kargil war Vajpayee's finest hour, but it also showcased his strategic understanding in the manner in which he transformed the initial setback into a strategic victory for India.

The role that the Indian Navy played during the Kargil war had left a strong impression on Prime Minister Vajpayee and I do believe that it largely influenced his novel approach in how to deal with China by using India's strategic advantage at sea to offset the tactical problems we face on the land border. In dealing with China he was never on the back foot and it was certainly a refreshing change from the demeaning manner in which India had been kowtowing to China for decades.

This book is my first-hand account of my tenure as a Navy Chief who served with Prime Minister Vajpayee and it is based entirely on my personal experiences and interaction with him. This is not a biography of Prime Minister Vajpayee, nor is it in any manner of speaking an analysis of his statecraft or an insight into his political acumen.

This is simply a distilled impression of what Prime Minister Vajpayee meant to the armed forces, as remembered by one of the Chiefs who served with him at the turn of the new millennium. However, the deep impression that has been with me of the Vajpayee era, has been placed on record in the final part of my presentation as the 'Vajpayee Legacy'.

This memoir is a tribute to Atal Bihari Vajpayee's greatness which is perhaps best summed up in a poetic depiction by Rudyard Kipling that follows.

Admiral Sushil Kumar
Former Chief of the Indian Navy (1998–2001)

IF

If you can keep your head when all about you
Are losing theirs and blaming it on you,
If you can trust yourself when all men doubt you,
But make allowance for their doubting too;
If you can wait and not be tired by waiting,
Or being lied about, don't deal in lies,
Or being hated, don't give way to hating,
And yet don't look too good, nor talk too wise:

If you can dream—and not make dreams your master;
If you can think—and not make thoughts your aim;
If you can meet with Triumph and Disaster
And treat those two impostors just the same;
If you can bear to hear the truth you've spoken
Twisted by knaves to make a trap for fools,
Or watch the things you gave your life to, broken,
And stoop and build 'em up with worn-out tools:

If you can make one heap of all your winnings
And risk it on one turn of pitch-and-toss,
And lose, and start again at your beginnings
And never breathe a word about your loss;
If you can force your heart and nerve and sinew
To serve your turn long after they are gone,
And so hold on when there is nothing in you
Except the Will which says to them: 'Hold on!'
If you can talk with crowds and keep your virtue,
Or walk with Kings—nor lose the common touch,
If neither foes nor loving friends can hurt you,
If all men count with you, but none too much;
If you can fill the unforgiving minute
With sixty seconds' worth of distance run,
Yours is the Earth and everything that's in it,
And—which is more—you'll be a Man, my son!

Rudyard Kipling

ACKNOWLEDGEMENTS

It is not easy to precisely reconstruct operational events and experiences that happened two decades ago, but with the help of military colleagues, my task was simplified. I, therefore, record my appreciation for General Ved Malik, General S.Padmanabhan, Admiral Madhvendra Singh, Admiral Arun Prakash and Air Chief Marshal Anil Tipnis. Their help was invaluable.

Admiral Suresh Bangara, an erudite scholar in defence matters and strategic affairs, has greatly helped in refining my presentation and I must also single out Admiral Ganesh Mahadevan, whose evergreen talent for sketching has added a touch of spice for a special chapter that highlights the lighter side of Prime Minister Vajpayee and life in the Navy.

Being my maiden attempt at writing a book, an instant feedback was essential and I could not have found a better person than my batchmate Admiral Davy Das, whose no-holds-barred critique removed many of the cobwebs from my script.

From running a Navy to writing a book is indeed a far cry. So most importantly, I must acknowledge the overarching support of Konark Publishers and thank Managing Director K.P.R. Nair and his team of professionals. The painstaking effort and invaluable contribution of Coordinating Editor Jiza Joy, Manuscript Editor Dipali Singh and Book and Cover Designer Misha Oberoi have greatly helped to meet the target date for the twentieth anniversary of the Kargil war, which I have always considered to be Prime Minister Vajpayee's finest hour.

Finally, I must admit that there is a huge difference between military writing and journalistic prose and in this respect, I must acknowledge the role of my wife, whose Master's degree in English Literature was certainly of enormous help. Without much ado, Venita quietly scanned through my drafts and cut out the pompous military jargon that *faujis* often get attuned to. I must say it certainly helps to have a soulmate as a sounding board 24x7 though it may not be the finest thing for one's ego.

'History is the biography of Great Men'

Thomas Carlyle – Circa 1840

PART I

THE VAJPAYEE YEARS

CHAPTER 1

THE SPRING OF 1999: KARGIL BEGINS

When the history of the Kargil war is finally recorded and analysed, future generations will realise the huge impact of Prime Minister Vajpayee on the conduct of this war and how he projected the armed forces as an instrument of state power. It was a classical lesson in the art of statecraft.

•

HOW IT ALL BEGAN...

It was in the spring of 1999 that it all began and I recall this initial phase quite clearly as I was officiating as the Chairman of the Chiefs of Staff Committee (COSC) since Army Chief General Ved Malik was abroad on an assignment.

The reports that first came in were quite vague and hazy.

They alluded to stray incidents along the Line of Control (LoC) with Pakistan, such as a report that an Indian army patrol that had not returned from a survey and how shepherds had seen suspicious-looking strangers on our side of the LoC. Despite the uncertain information, Vice Chief of Army Staff Lieutenant General Chandrashekhar was understandably concerned and requested an immediate armed reconnaissance by the Air Force. But Air Chief Marshal Tipnis quite rightly advised against this, saying that hastily inducting the Indian Air Force could send the wrong signal. With only scanty reports available, the situation was confused and seemed to be only a minor border incident in an area that had always been regarded as no man's land.

By the time General Malik returned from his trip abroad, the situation was clear. It was neither a stray border incident nor was it the handiwork of *jihadis*. Something sinister was obviously afoot as the intruders had entrenched themselves on our side of the LoC in well-fortified bunkers sited at strategically commanding locations. Intelligence sources confirmed the involvement of Pakistan's army with General Pervez Musharraf as the villain of the piece. This manoeuvre had obviously been executed over a well-calculated time frame and Pakistan's treachery had squarely caught us off guard. It was duplicity because it was only in February of the same year that Prime Minister Vajpayee and his Pakistani counterpart Nawaz Sharif had signed the Lahore Accord, pledging to coexist peacefully, avoid conflict, and stand by a mutual understanding that Pakistan and India were committed to nuclear disarmament. It was internationally welcomed as a sign that the strained relationship between the two countries was improving.

VAJPAYEE'S RESPONSE

Deeply concerned by the evidence of this perfidy from across the border by a country he had recently visited, with his hand outstretched in friendship, Prime Minister Vajpayee galvanised the Cabinet Committee on Security (CCS) into action and issued a clear-cut directive to the armed forces: 'Evict the intruders, but do not cross the LoC!'

'*Not crossing the LoC*' was a serious operational handicap for our armed forces but the Prime Minister stuck to his decision. He knew that a war between adversaries with nuclear capability could have disastrous consequences and his insistence on 'strategic restraint' paid off in full measure. It garnered massive international support, and more importantly, it ensured that the war would be fought on terms dictated by India. This indeed was Prime Minister Vajpayee's masterstroke which paved the way for a strategic victory at Kargil.

PAKISTAN'S VULNERABILITY

By early June 1999, as our Army and Air Force were preparing for combat operations on the LoC, task forces of the Indian Navy's Western Fleet had swiftly deployed and seized the initiative in the North Arabian Sea.

Very well briefed, the Prime Minister was aware that Pakistan's lifeline lay at sea, its vital oil supply having to be ferried in bulky tankers across the oceans. With the Indian Navy taking the initiative, the task forces were already astride

Pakistan's jugular. This would certainly prevent escalation and confine the conflict to the LoC.

Within a few days, Pakistan realised how seriously vulnerable it was and began escorting its oil tankers at sea. When I reported this development at the next meeting of the CCS, the Prime Minister's quiet smile conveyed his satisfaction, for it showed that the pressure tactics of what is termed 'coercive diplomacy' had put Pakistan on the defensive.

PRECAUTIONARY STAGE

By the end of June, 1999, as operations on the Himalayan heights at Tololing and Tiger Hill reached a climax, tension mounted as desperate Pakistani Generals threatened nuclear retaliation. At a COSC meeting of the armed forces' Chiefs on 18 June 1999, General Ved Malik issued an advisory for our armed forces: **'Be prepared for war—whether declared or otherwise'**.

The Indian Navy's combined Western and Eastern Fleets were poised for combat and the Prime Minister had been continuously briefed about our Navy's deployment. With Defence Minister George Fernandes kept in the loop, there was confidence in the CCS that the overwhelming superiority of our Navy to Pakistan's Navy, would have a sobering effect on Pakistan. And the media reflected this confidence. For instance, a headline in *Hindustan Times* read: **'Alert Indian Navy helped pin down Pakistan in Kargil'**.

With an escalation imminent, the situation radically altered, particularly for the Indian Navy whose task forces were positioned at strategic choke points in the Arabian Sea. Being an international waterway, with neutrals present, the 'precautionary stage' for war was thus an important threshold for our Navy, as the Rules of Engagement (ROE), which define any unacceptable provocative action or use of force, needed to be applied in accordance with the international maritime convention.

The Defence Minister accordingly arranged an urgent meeting with External Affairs Minister Jaswant Singh and National Security Adviser Brajesh Mishra. Apart from the ROE, which are basically for self-defence, I also explained the implications of a Maritime Exclusion Zone (MEZ) to prevent unauthorised entry of civilians in a naval zone, as was done during the Falklands War of 1982.

Having been adequately briefed before the CCS meeting, Prime Minister Vajpayee readily appreciated the Navy's request for enforcing the ROE in the northern Arabian Sea. In his inimitable and confident manner, the Prime Minister nodded his approval and with his green signal, the Indian Navy flashed the code word for Operation Talwar. And so it was that the operation began, aiming to blockade Pakistani ports and cut off its sea trade as well as the routes that Pakistan used to convey imported supplies of much-needed oil and fuel.

As designated task forces of the Indian Navy commenced advancing forward, our monitoring stations intercepted a Pakistan Navy signal, which surprisingly, was uncoded. It was from Pakistan's Navy headquarters to Pakistani warships with the message: **'Remain in harbour'**.

Navies worldwide have a professional understanding amongst themselves and are conscious of their role and potential. And since they always operate in international waters with other

Navies also present, they know how to keep their distance. This is in contrast to the situation at the LoC. That was the interpretation I gave at the CCS meeting for the Pakistani Navy's message that we had intercepted.

It evoked keen interest and triggered an animated discussion, with Prime Minister Vajpayee finally breaking into his characteristic smile and adding with a poetic flourish: '*Perhaps Pakistan's Navy wanted nothing to do with General Musharraf's Himalayan folly*!'

The media reported this development with exuberance. *Jane's International Weekly's* headline, for example, commended the Navy with: **'Indian Navy muscle hastened end to border fight'**

8

THE VAJPAYEE IMPACT

Following the Lahore Accord of February 1999, Pakistan's treachery at Kargil was a setback but the armed forces bounced back and the war ended with India's victory. Their valour and sacrifice had done the nation proud and accolades were heaped on the armed forces. But 'in the fog of war', the larger picture sometimes goes unnoticed. And so was the pivotal role played by Prime Minister Vajpayee. His was a stellar contribution but remains blurred in the background—perhaps a reflection of his own modest and unassuming character.

SYNERGISING THE ARMED FORCES

When the chips were down, it was Vajpayee's iron will and positive approach that galvanised the armed forces to combat a well-entrenched enemy on the icy Himalayan heights where incredible feats of valour and sacrifice by our jawans and officers brought glory to the nation. This synergy that he infused into our fighting forces, ultimately transformed a tactical loss into a strategic victory for India.

Though Kargil happened two decades ago, the manner in which he synergised and motivated our armed forces is testified by the messages that remain on record. For instance, I sent the following message:

Naval Headquarters: 5 July 1999

Personal for: Chief of Army Staff and Chief of Air Staff

With admiration and pride all ranks of the Indian Navy salute our Army and Air Force for their stunning feats at Kargil under daunting conditions. And now your capping success at Tiger Hill says it all.

As we guard the seaward flank, the Indian Navy is inspired and motivated by the intrepid action of our comrades in arms.

Good hunting and God bless…

Admiral Sushil Kumar

•

General Malik conveyed his thanks:

Army Headquarters

Personal for Chief of the Naval Staff

Dear Sushil,

Thank you for your warm appreciation of the performance of our officers and jawans at Kargil. Your message gives us the encouragement to carry on our endeavour until every intruder is evicted.

Your warning to the Pakistani Navy has been an extremely useful contribution. The enemy is fully aware that he faces the synergised effort of the Indian armed forces.

With warm regards,
General Ved Malik

PERSONAL RAPPORT

The Prime Minister had an uncanny instinct by which he felt the pulse of the armed forces, but to get to know the forces better, he institutionalised a procedure for the Chiefs of the Army, Navy, and Air Force to meet him regularly at his residence. Since he was a man of few words, it was difficult to fathom his thoughts for he hardly spoke at this weekly interaction. It was the Chiefs who did all the talking, generally about our military life in the forward areas. He seemed to have an earnest desire to understand this facet of the Indian armed forces. Strategy and tactics were never discussed during this interaction.

Through his personal touch, Prime Minister Vajpayee established an emotional bond that infused synergy into the

PARTNERS in VICTORY: At a formal reception after the Kargil war, Prime Minister Vajpayee is seen seated (with his back to the camera) sharing a few light moments with his military chiefs standing (from left to right) Admiral Sushil Kumar, Air Chief Marshal Anil Tipnis and General Ved Malik.

The author and Air Chief Marshal Anil Tipnis at a formal function.

us a vital lesson. It highlighted the serious systemic drawbacks that pointed to the urgent need to operationally and logistically integrate the three armed forces and establish a military chain of command and control that should be in consonance with the challenging requirements of modern warfare.

•

THE KARGIL IMBROGLIO

In military terms, it can never be denied that Kargil caught us completely by surprise. That was the ground reality and the primary reason why Prime Minister Vajpayee constituted the Kargil Review Committee (KRC) under the chairmanship of the erudite defence expert, K. Subrahmanyam. He had a wide charter and his terms of reference were to examine internal security, coastal security, and the overarching system of defence management in India.

It was the Committee on Defence Management headed by Arun Singh who had been the Minister of State for Defence in Rajiv Gandhi's cabinet that drew the attention of the government to the vital need for operationally and logistically integrating the three armed forces with a well-defined military chain of command. This change had become necessary since the concept of military operations had radically altered over the years and major armed forces in the world, such as those of the US and the UK had already been reconfigured to meet the changing requirements of modern warfare. On the other hand, the Indian armed forces, which are considered to be the fourth largest in the world, have not been able to shed their single-service mindset nor their tradition-bound ways that go back to colonial times.

For command and control, the Indian armed forces still function in accordance with the Chiefs of Staff Committee (COSC) system, which is a relic of the British Raj, dating back to 1924. While the British themselves have long since replaced it with the Chief of Defence Staff (CDS) model, we still hang on to the COSC system. Quite strangely, some people within the Indian armed forces and outside too, believe that there is nothing wrong with the COSC system.

Having been through the Kargil conflict as one of the armed forces' Chiefs, I must admit that it was mainly the sheer grit and indomitable courage of our front line units that turned the odds in our favour. Considering the lack of a robust command and control framework, I hate to visualise the consequences had this border clash escalated into full-blown hostilities, with the Chinese opening up a second front.

It may only be a footnote in history but is worth remembering, that our intelligence sources had confirmed that General Musharraf had been camping in Beijing, desperately making overtures to the Chinese. That was the time when the situation was getting too hot for his Generals and defeat was staring them in the face.

THE LACUNA THAT EXISTS

The COSC is an anachronism and an apology for a military command and control system for warfare in this day and age.

Having been the chairman of the COSC for close to two years, I came to realise that it is an outmoded structure that has a vague operational charter. It is just not equipped to handle the strategic situation that we are confronted with today. We need a robust command and control arrangement and not a system like the COSC, which is more like a cooperative arrangement where the priority for each service Chief is his own parish.

In the 1971 war, the then Army Chief, the charismatic Sam Manekshaw had carried the day and it was fortuitous that during the Kargil conflict, the three service Chiefs had been together from their training days. But fighting a modern war cannot be left to chance or camaraderie alone.

Egoism is a human trait and the Indian armed forces are not immune to turf war. It was the bitter inter-service rivalry during the Vietnam War that had prompted the US government to take a hard look at their military structure. Thereafter, a series of catastrophic military failures led to the US policymakers enacting the Goldwater–Nichols Act, which radically reformed the system in 1986 by restructuring and streamlining the US military's command chain. The chairman of the US Joint Chiefs of Staff (CJCS) and his team now exercises operational control of theatre commands.

SITUATION ALONG THE LAC

Having to cater for a two-front war with nuclear armed adversaries requires split-second decision-making that can ensure coordinated action. It is for this reason that single-point command and control with the resources of the three armed forces systematically integrated has become operationally imperative.

Since 2015, the mammoth-sized Chinese armed forces have been revamped into six integrated theatre commands. With this major military reform, the Peoples' Liberation Army (PLA) has further strengthened its position along the lengthy 4057-kilometre Line of Actual Control (LAC), while we continue to remain on the defensive, ever since the 1962 debacle, when we lost the border conflict with China.

The LAC meanders across the territories of five Indian states—Kashmir, Uttarakhand, Himachal Pradesh, Sikkim and Arunachal Pradesh. During my tenure as the Chairman of the COSC, I had the opportunity to visit some of our forward areas along the LAC and realised how we are bogged down and hampered by poor connectivity. Added to that, we now find ourselves further disadvantaged after the Chinese have refined their order of battle. We are in a strange predicament where the Indian Army and Air Force have as many as seven operational commands and formations arrayed against one single integrated theatre command of the PLA with its clear-cut command and control system. Since none of our operational formations have their headquarters or operations centres co-located, our command and control system remains disjointed, placing us at a further disadvantage. All this could be intimidating, as the Chinese now have a distinct advantage for manoeuvre warfare along our Himalayan border.

In the past, we have been left bewildered and flat-footed by the defiant and repeated Chinese incursions. Now with the Chinese unified command system well in place, it is high time that we seriously introspected and got our own act together.

A STEP IN THE RIGHT DIRECTION

It is reassuring that this sort of anomaly has been mainly removed in the case of our Strategic Forces Command (SFC) which controls our nuclear combat resources. The SFC is now an integrated system with a clear mandate and was brought into force in 2003 after India declared its 'No First Use' nuclear doctrine. With the sea-based nuclear deterrent firmly in place, Admiral Vijay Shankar of the Navy took over as the Commander-in-Chief of the SFC in 2006 and when the SFC moved to its permanent location, Admiral S.P.S. Cheema was placed in command as its Commander-in Chief. However, the military chain of command for the SFC still passes via the COSC, which has its own systemic inadequacies.

While the SFC has been an important step in the right direction and is well structured for nuclear deterrence, the larger problem still exists with our conventional warfare capability.

CONVENTIONAL CAPABILITY

The conventional forces of the Indian Army, Navy, and Air Force are spread across the length and breadth of the subcontinent and remain in their old-fashioned configuration. Each arm of the military continues to operate in a single-service mode, seeking pre-eminence in its own sphere of control—land, the sea and air.

We thus have a situation where the conventional capability of the Indian armed forces is disjointed, with the Army, Navy, and Air Force manning their own respective operations centres. This effectively means that the three members of the COSC are solely in charge of their own service operations. This handicap could cost the nation dearly, since it is conventional wars that are meant to be fought. This has been the rationale for creating the Chief of Defence Staff system (as in the UK) or the Chairman of the Joint Chiefs of Staff (as in the US).

The nuclear deterrent is certainly needed but it has to be matched alongside by a credible conventional capability. While nuclear deterrence is *subjective*, it is conventional deterrence that really matters as it not only prevents full-scale hostilities, but if the need arises, ensures a credible response in our favour. This was aptly demonstrated by Prime Minister Vajpayee's strategic restraint during the Kargil war when he called the bluff of the desperate Generals across the border, who threatened nuclear retaliation.

THE FOLLOW-UP

With the acceptance of the Kargil Committee Report, the committees set up by the Group of Ministers (GoM) were closely monitored by Prime Minister Vajpayee. These committees had a wide interaction with several agencies in the armed forces and received a continuous feedback from the COSC.

The idea of creating the Andaman and Nicobar Command (ANC) was first injected by Admiral Ravi Ganesh who had earlier served as the Fortress Commander of the Andaman and Nicobar (FORTAN). This was a tri-services organisation under the Navy and had the basic ingredients for a theatre command. This was the first major recommendation to the GoM and was readily accepted as an experiment aiming towards the long-term goal of integrating all the 19 commands of the armed forces. That is how the post of the Commander-in-Chief of the Andaman and Nicobar (CINCAN) was formed, with it being a rotational appointment tenable by the Army, Navy, or Air Force.

Predictably, as also occurred in the US and the UK, there was resistance to further change, both from within the armed forces and outside too. Admittedly, the philosophy of integrated theatre commands has to be necessarily different as tri-service concerns need an overriding priority. This is not possible in the existing system where the three service Chiefs exercise complete and absolute control over their respective service. However in the unified model, the three service Chiefs would continue to have major responsibilities such as raising, training, equipping and providing combat-ready platforms for operational deployment by the CDS. This may partially erode the operational role of the existing Army, Navy and Air Force Chiefs as the CDS would singly exercise direct operational control of the theatre commands. For this functional role, the CDS has to be deemed as the *first among equals*. This has become inevitable in the overriding interest of the nation's security and therefore, in countries that have major armed forces, this much-needed reform has been brought in through legislation.

Besides the concerns of a few individuals within the armed forces, the creation of a CDS also seems to have got our *babu*s worried. What matters most to the bureaucracy is their equivalence with other institutions and the military has always been their main obsession. By law, the CDS would become the Principal Adviser to the Prime Minister and Defence Minister. Perhaps this may have had a dreaded connotation for the bureaucracy, as their 'hold' on the Defence Minister may diminish. This may well be why the proposal for a CDS which was the foremost recommendation by the GoM, got quietly shelved in the *Yes Minister* style.

A BOGEY WITHIN

Quite apart from the impediments mentioned earlier, there is an unspoken bogey that sometimes confuses the insecure politician in India. It has always been apparent that lurking somewhere deep within the system is an irrational phobia about the military establishment posing a challenge to civilian authority. The sordid examples of military coups in our neighbourhood have compounded these misperceptions and have also led to an uneasy civil–military relationship.

Prime Minister Vajpayee had addressed this issue squarely since he was convinced of the professionalism and dedication of our armed forces. But despite his best efforts, the much-needed reforms for our antiquated military structure could not be achieved during the Vajpayee era.

THE KARGIL LESSON

The Kargil Review Committee was constituted by the government to analyse the weaknesses, both systemic and organisationally in the armed forces of India. It was indeed a timely measure since we had not been tested since the 1971 war with Pakistan. Consequently the GoM, under the watchful eyes of Prime

Minister Vajpayee, closely monitored the implementation of the recommendations of the expert committees. By 2002, I had retired from service but was sanguine that all the recommendations would be implemented expeditiously.

However, due to reasons best known to the government, the creation of the CDS, integrated theatre commands and integration of the Ministry of Defence (MoD) with the service headquarters could not be completed before the elections in 2004.

The admiration for Prime Minister Vajpayee would have redoubled had these remaining reforms been implemented during his tenure. But it was not to be and with the change of governments, the impetus was lost and with the priorities having changed, the status quo prevailed.

If India is serious about improving the war-fighting capabilities of its armed forces, the modus vivendi can only be through a political mandate. The government in power would need to take the bull by the horns as was done in the US, with the Goldwater—Nichols Act of 1986.

CHAPTER 3

BRIDGING THE GAP IN CIVIL–MILITARY RELATIONS

The civil–military divide is a phenomenon which afflicts democratic nations that maintain large-sized armed forces. Although in India it has always been a chronic problem, it was somehow glossed over.

While the contours of civil–military relations may vary with every country, the problem is universal. This has always been the most significant factor to be considered in our context, since India faces a dual challenge—inimical neighbours to contend with and a chronic insurgency within our borders. Handling civil–military relations in India has accordingly, been a complex task, the controversy with the Armed Forces Special Powers Act, which confers special powers to the Indian armed forces in 'disturbed areas', being a case in point. The criticism of this Act is that human rights violations in these areas have allegedly taken place.

VAJPAYEE'S CONCERN

It was during the private interactions of the armed forces' Chiefs with Prime Minister Vajpayee that his concerns became evident. He seemed keen to settle the unresolved debate on how civil–military relations ought to be handled in India.

Having personally seen the performance of our armed forces during the Kargil war, the Prime Minister was convinced of their professionalism and dedication. He was also aware that with their apolitical character and secular credentials, our armed forces were seen as a strong pillar of Indian society and admired by our discerning populace.

In the past, the crisis in civil–military relations was simply regarded as a *fait accompli* and conveniently ignored. But it was not so for Prime Minister Vajpayee. His was an open mind with a positive approach and he wanted to address the problem squarely.

THE FAULT LINES

The problem of interfacing the military with civil society goes back to antiquity—to the days of Sun Tzu, the Chinese general and military strategist in about the fifth century BCE and Kautilya, who wrote the *Arthashastra* on statecraft in the third century BCE—when it came to be realised that handling the army called for astute statecraft. In the Indian context, our civil–military relations are a by-product of our colonial history as well as deep-rooted traditions.

What has never been recognised is that this relationship exists on fault lines that stem from misperceptions and rigid beliefs, which have calcified over the years. Added to that are the sordid examples of military coups in our immediate neighbourhood, which have compounded the situation. The fallout is an uneasy relationship tinged with mistrust on either side of the institutional divide.

It has always been apparent that somewhere deep within the system, lurks an irrational phobia about the Indian military establishment posing a challenge to civilian authority. Apart from that, the armed forces have always had to contend with the ambitious designs of the bureaucracy, for whom what finally matters is its equation and equivalence with other institutions. As the military has always been its main obsession, this has certainly widened the gap in civil–military relations.

Curiously, the long overdue reform to integrate the Indian armed forces with the Chief of Defence Staff (CDS) system appears to have been quietly scuttled—but that is another story.

MILITARY ETHOS

Understanding the Indian military subculture has always been a complex matter and the lack of this understanding has perhaps been the primary cause of the disjointed relationship that has always existed between the armed forces and their civilian political superiors.

What had never been realised or accepted is that although the military is part of the society it serves, the soldier is not just a civilian in uniform. On the contrary, the soldier belongs to a breed that has its own ethos. And this ethos necessarily has to be different for members of the armed forces to succeed in the dangerous situations they face, circumstances that differ greatly from civilian life. This is the crux of the problem that plagues civil–military relations across the globe.

A long time ago, this sentiment had resonated in the *Arthashastra*, where Kautilya advised the Mauryan Emperor Chandragupta:

'While the Magadha citizenry endeavours to make the state prosper, the Mauryan soldier guarantees that the state continues to exist.

He is the silent sine qua non *of our very being.'*

VAJPAYEE'S INTUITION

Prime Minister Vajpayee was well versed in Kautilya's treatise, but he had his own intuitive mind. He had discerned the striking difference between the ways of the Indian armed forces and those in civilian authority.

To a military person, a target means only two things—you can either hit it or miss it. But to a *neta* or *babu,* a target has many interpretations. It is something that can be ignored, extended, or manipulated.

The Prime Minister was also conscious of the unquestioned loyalty and legendary sacrifices of our armed forces, be it in natural disasters, insurgency, or war. Who else could have been tasked for Operation Blue Star to flush out militants from the

Golden Temple or to suppress the police unrest in the 1960s?

This was the paradox that confronted Prime Minister Vajpayee when the Kargil crisis erupted, but he saw in this an opportunity to address the festering problem of civil–military relations.

INDUCING CONFIDENCE

The ultimate need is to induce confidence in the civil–military relationship and create an environment of trust. But in the past there never was an institutionalised approach to address the civil–military divide.

As mentioned earlier, Prime Minister Vajpayee had set up a framework for regular and private interaction with his armed forces' Chiefs—General Ved Malik, Air Chief Marshal Tipnis and myself. His aim was clear and obviously had a twofold purpose. Firstly, it was to gain the confidence of the armed forces and ensure that they remain focused and motivated for the developing warlike situation on the Line of Control (LOC). Secondly, he wanted to know more about our military ethos, as he knew that this was the key to civil–military relations.

It was this kind of understanding that showed how sound his political leadership was. Though the catalyst for his thoughtful approach had been the Kargil war, it was no flash in the pan. In the years that followed the Kargil war, it was under his leadership that 'pulling together' had become the norm. With his personal touch, the Prime Minister kept his flock together and also bridged the gap in the civil–military divide. For us, the armed forces' Chiefs, his unique approach was an eye-opener.

CHAPTER 4

FIRST INTERNATIONAL FLEET REVIEW: *BRIDGES OF FRIENDSHIP*

It was the end of January 2001 and India's first International Fleet Review (IFR) was about to commence. In this mega event being hosted for the very first time in India, 30 Navies from across the globe were to participate. It was planned to be held in the new millennium and the Mumbai harbour was the venue. But as fate would have it, it was at this very time, just as foreign warships were en route to India, that a massive earthquake struck Gujarat. The disaster cast a pall of gloom over the nation.

All eyes were on Prime Minister Vajpayee for his decision—to go ahead with the IFR or not? And this is how it all happened…

●

Conducting an in-house review on a national scale was always a major evolution that required long-term planning and massive coordination. But the very thought of hosting an IFR only underscored how almost impossible it was. Comparable to organising a mini-Olympics, the sheer scale of logistics in an IFR would be mind-boggling.

When I took command of the Indian Navy, it had struck me that my tenure would span the Navy's transition into the next millennium. It was to match this important milestone that I toyed with the idea of conducting an IFR.

As I contemplated this daunting task, I also had a different thought in mind—could this be a way for the people of India to know what their Navy is all about? It would be reassuring for them to know that ours was the only Navy in the Indian Ocean region that has the capability to operate aircraft carrier battle groups and nuclear submarines.

I had always felt that the maritime character of our country had been overshadowed by an overbearing continental mindset. The problems along the LoC and the McMahon Line demarcating India and China had given us a landward fixation. It was perhaps an operational imperative but in the process, it had eclipsed the maritime dimension of India, which lay at the opposite end of the subcontinent. In a manner of speaking, the Navy of India seemed out of sight and somewhere over the horizon. It was in this context that it occurred to me that a mega event such as an IFR could perhaps showcase the Indian Navy to the people of India.

Conducting such a major event seemed incalculably difficult and was undoubtedly going to be an extremely challenging task. But I was greatly encouraged by the spontaneous response from my three Commanders-in-Chief—Admiral Madhvendra Singh, Admiral Vinod Pasricha and Admiral Ravi Ganesh.

CATASTROPHE STRIKES

Realising the potential of naval diplomacy, Prime Minister Vajpayee saw in this mega maritime event, a great opportunity to reach out internationally. And with his concurrence, the theme for the IFR was conceptualised as the 'Bridges of Friendship'. It was scheduled two years hence for mid-February 2001 and preparations went ahead in full swing.

Several foreign warships were already on their way to Mumbai when the massive earthquake of 26 January 2001 rocked Gujarat and its adjacent coastal regions, causing devastation of catastrophic proportions. The shock waves were felt almost 1,000 km from the epicentre at Bhuj in central Gujarat. With more than 20,000 people instantly killed and millions injured and rendered homeless, this disaster was a national calamity.

The conduct of India's first IFR hung in balance.

THE DILEMMA

Only a few major Navies of the world, such as those of the US and the UK, occasionally conduct IFRs. India was on the verge of joining that special league, when the Gujarat disaster struck the nation. An IFR has always been regarded as a formal military function. It is traditionally conducted with great dignity and ceremony where the head of state of the host nation formally reviews the assembled armada of multinational warships.

There was less than a week left for this international event to commence and some of the foreign warships had already arrived at the Mumbai harbour, even as national mourning swamped the country. Although an IFR is conducted with military precision and graced with sobriety and dignity, there is no doubt that the pomp and splendour of such an event would have a celebratory touch to it.

What would the nation feel about such an IFR being held when it had yet to come to terms with the Gujarat tragedy. This was the dilemma that faced the Indian Navy and the Government of India. And all eyes were on Prime Minister Vajpayee. He had to take the call.

EXECUTIVE DECISION

The pros and cons of the IFR were discussed threadbare at a crucial CCS meeting chaired by Prime Minister Vajpayee with his senior cabinet ministers present. Defence Minister George Fernandes explained that the Navy had already planned to cancel some of the associated carnival type of activities which could be out of sync with the mood of the nation. Since 30 nations were involved and several foreign warships had already arrived, Foreign Minister Jaswant Singh was of the view that the IFR ought to be held, as it was essentially a military function.

Assorted views of others present were voiced at this meeting and Prime Minister Vajpayee listened patiently. He was in a pensive mood and finally unveiled his thoughts to give his executive decision, the gist of which was: *The tragedy that India has faced is known to the whole world; let them also know that we can face up to such a challenge. The show must go on.*

Top: Prime Minister Atal Bihari Vajpayee is all set to view the First International Fleet Review at Mumbai in February 2001.

Prime Minister Vajpayee being welcomed by the author for the First International Fleet Review at Mumbai in February 2001. Also seen is Defence Minister George Fernandes.

Prime Minister Vajpayee meeting the chiefs of foreign Navies during India's First International Fleet Review.

During the first International Fleet Review at Mumbai in February 2001, the Supreme Commander of our armed forces President K.R. Narayanan is seen along with Navy Chief Admiral Sushil Kumar (left) and Vice Admiral Madhvendra Singh, FOC-in-C, Western Naval Command. In the background is the Indian Navy's Flagship INS *Viraat*.

For dealing with China, Prime Minister Vajpayee focused on building the strategic capability of the Indian Navy. (Mentioned in Chapter 5)

The Indian Navy's strategic capability includes the sea-based nuclear deterrent.

INS *Vikramaditya* and its battle group warships have transformed the strategic landscape in the Indian Ocean.

The Cutting Edge of the Indian Navy.

BRIDGES OF FRIENDSHIP

Saturday, 17 February 2001, thus got etched in the annals of India's maritime history. That was the day on which the Indian Navy announced its arrival into the new millennium, with the conduct of the first IFR ever held in India.

IFR 2001 will be long remembered for its seminal character. It was distinctive for many reasons. It was the first such national event to be held in the new millennium and reflected the many sinews of national prowess. Dressed up in their ceremonial best, the international fleet of warships was reviewed by K.R. Narayanan, the President of India, accompanied by Prime Minister Vajpayee.

In keeping with India's abiding commitment to peace and the tenets of global good order, this IFR held under the overarching theme of 'Bridges of Friendship' and the coming together of most of the major Navies of the world, symbolized the common desire for cooperative security and conflict prevention. Yet in an unspoken way, this event reflected India's new relevance in the post-cold war regional strategic calculus as also the significance of India's maritime dimension, with the Indian Navy as a key player.

Decades later, as I look back at India's first IFR of 2001, I wonder if it would ever have been possible if the Prime Minister had been someone other than Atal Bihari Vajpayee. He had the vision and the will to make it happen....

CHAPTER 5

DEALING WITH CHINA: THE VAJPAYEE WAY

The Chinese debacle of 1962 is history and the military equation between India and China has significantly altered since then, with both Asian giants being armed with nuclear weapons as well. Yet the defiant Chinese intrusions across the Line of Actual Control (LAC) have not ceased and India has always remained on the back foot.

While concerned by this worrisome trend, what had greatly intrigued Prime Minister Vajpayee was the vastly different situation that prevailed at sea between the Chinese PLA Navy and the Indian Navy, as compared with the tense situation on the land border between the PLA and the Indian Army.

While the two armies cautiously patrolled the LAC, there has always been a healthy relationship and a professional understanding between the Navies. For several years, our warships have been conducting joint exercises with the Chinese Navy in the China Sea and goodwill visits by our Eastern Fleet to Chinese ports and the recent participation in their International Fleet Reviews (IFRs) at Qingdao has been a regular feature.

This contrasting situation at the problematic land border as compared with the normal atmosphere on the maritime front, has never been understood by India's strategic planners and diplomatically too, it has been regarded as lopsided. What has never been appreciated is that this asymmetrical situation has a lot to do with the geographical and strategic advantage that India has in the Indian Ocean Region (IOR). Sitting astride China's energy lifeline has always given India the upper hand on the maritime front.

It is well known that the modern world was reshaped through naval power and that India was actually colonised from seaward by superior naval forces. But India suffers from a continental mindset that is reminiscent of the Napoleonic era and in this strange psychological milieu, historical evidence hardly matters. So the maritime logic propounded for centuries, from Sun Tzu to Alfred Thayer Mahan, the American naval strategist, historian, and theorist, is just a footnote—*to be secure on land, one has to be strong at sea.*

History also reminds us why the Greeks of antiquity and the emperors of ancient Rome went about building their Navies even though it was an era of continental wars. On the other hand, leaders like Alexander, Napoleon, and Hitler failed the test of sea power, as they never understood the purpose of a Navy.

Prime Minister Vajpayee's understanding of what a Navy is all about was triggered by what he had personally experienced during the Kargil war. Well before our Army and Air Force had swung into action to evict the intruders along the LOC, the Indian Navy had swiftly deployed and seized the initiative from seaward. With powerful task forces of the Indian Navy sitting astride her energy lifeline, Pakistan's vulnerability lay exposed at sea.

This strategic manoeuvre of the Indian Navy seemed to have left a strong impression on Prime Minister Vajpayee and in my personal view it was this experience of the Kargil war that had a bearing on the innovative approach that Prime Minister Vajpayee subsequently adopted in dealing with China. It was certainly a refreshing change from the demeaning manner in which India had been timidly dealing with China for decades.

OUR LAND-CENTRIC MINDSET

Scarred by the 1962 debacle and the defiant Chinese intrusions across the LAC, an inferiority complex had kept us feeling at a disadvantage. So obsessed were we with the LAC and the McMahon Line, that our geopolitical attention got riveted to the Himalayan border. This obsession turned into a mindset that was so land-centric that we simply failed to comprehend that India and China were also maritime neighbours, with vital waterways that were of great strategic significance.

More significantly, what had never been realised by our strategic planners, is that India always had a strategic advantage at sea and China was quite conscious of it.

CHINA'S SECURITY CONCERNS

From the turn of the century, it has been known that China's rapid growth has come at a huge cost. Being the largest consumer of energy in the world can be a dubious distinction for a country like China, whose gigantic requirement of crude oil has almost entirely to be imported from overseas. It has to be brought in massive super tankers from the Gulf or the Mediterranean, thousands of miles away. This is China's energy lifeline which has perforce to be routed via the Indian Ocean, where the Indian Navy exercises dominant sea control. The vulnerability of her energy lifeline has, therefore, drastically compounded China's security concerns.

China's dependence on the sea for its crude oil supply has been a major concern for decades and her immediate neighbours in the China Sea have been feeling the direct brunt of her desperate exertions. But of greatest concern to China is its Silk Route through the Indian Ocean Region (IOR) where the Indian Navy has the upper hand. China has, therefore, been conscious that its Achilles' heel lies precariously at sea in India's backyard.

Though China and India are maritime neighbours, their Navies operate in vastly different oceanic zones. The Pacific Ocean is where the PLA Navy is busy countering operational challenges, while the Indian Ocean has always been deemed as India's backyard. It is well known that China's professed claims in the China Sea have been bitterly disputed by her maritime neighbours. More importantly, her hostility towards major maritime powers, including the US, stems from her disregard for the right to innocent passage in the China Sea, in terms set down by the United Nations Convention on the Law of the Sea (UNCLOS).

India, on the other hand, has a geographical advantage in the Indian Ocean, with strategically located choke points such as the Straits of Malacca which is a vital waterway for China's energy lifeline.

With the Indian subcontinent positioned dominantly astride the sea lanes of communication, including China's new Silk Route, it is not India but China that finds itself on the back foot. The very thought of the energy lifeline being severed by the Indian Navy could be China's worst nightmare.

VAJPAYEE'S NOVEL APPROACH

It had become apparent to Prime Minister Vajpayee that this was an asymmetrical situation where India's operational advantage at sea over China had considerable potential for diplomatic leverage. Unlike the landward frontier with China, where we find ourselves tactically disadvantaged, the situation at sea is entirely in our favour as India has an immense geographical and strategic domination in the IOR. Prime Minister Vajpayee accordingly realised that the time was opportune to consider a change of tack from the disheartening manner in which we had been dealing with China.

Casting overboard the baggage of the past with its land-centric hangover, Prime Minister Vajpayee adopted a novel approach in dealing with China. In a manner of speaking, it was a 'naval' approach, where he gave an added fillip to building the Indian Navy's strategic capability.

It was during the Vajpayee era that a major emphasis was given to long-term strategic projects of the Indian Navy and significant among these was the induction of the powerful aircraft carrier battle group led by INS *Vikramaditya*. It has bolstered the Indian Navy's combat capability and transformed the strategic landscape of the IOR.

China has followed this development closely, as reports indicate that its very first aircraft carrier has yet to be inducted into operational service. It would be also aware that the Indian Navy's expertise in operating aircraft carriers goes back to the 1960s.

The need to operationally pool together the nuclear warfare resources of the Army, Navy, and Air Force was an important lesson that flowed out of the Kargil war of 1999. The Vajpayee government accordingly created the Strategic Forces Command (SFC) and in order to add muscle to India's nuclear deterrent, a major thrust was given to the Indian Navy's indigenous construction programme for SSBNs (ballistic missile submarines), and ICBMs (intercontinental ballistic missiles). This was a long-term project, which began in the mid-1980s.

The recent induction of India's first ICBM-firing nuclear submarine, INS *Arihant*, with other more potent SSBNs to follow, has been a major achievement. The strident message that it conveys is unlikely to be lost on China.

The tri-service integration of the Indian armed forces was the centre of an unresolved debate for decades and it was on the recommendation of the Kargil Review Committee (KRC) of 1999 that the Vajpayee government gave its approval to commence the process. A significant step in this direction was the creation of the Andaman and Nicobar Command (ANC, which has further reinforced India's maritime dominance in the Indian Ocean, since the Andaman and Nicobar Islands are strategically located at the mouth of the Malacca Straits, through which China's energy lifeline passes.

TESTING THE WATERS

A Navy's strategic role may require it to deploy to any part of the globe, where the interests of the nation so demand. Reach and endurance are accordingly important considerations for any blue water Navy.

To gauge the long-range capability of our Navy, a naval headquarters' operations team led by Admiral Suresh Bangara had coordinated a proposal with the Ministry of External Affairs (MEA). The plan was to deploy a task force of the Eastern Fleet comprising major surface combatants and submarines in the China Sea. This deployment was to be for an extended duration and included joint exercises with the Chinese Navy as well as a ceremonial visit to a major Chinese port.

I was disappointed, though not surprised, when I learnt from the grapevine that the Indian embassy in Beijing was of the view that this show of strength by the Indian Navy may not go down well with the Chinese authorities.

After bureaucratic discussions between the MEA and the Ministry of Defence (MoD) reached an impasse, I decided to raise the level and sought a meeting with Foreign Minister Jaswant Singh who advised us to discuss the matter with the Prime Minister.

At the meeting, I briefly explained to the Prime Minister

that the Chinese Navy deployed quite regularly in the Indian Ocean, which we consider to be our backyard. Prime Minister Vajpayee thought for a moment and unambiguously conveyed his decision, saying we were quite right and there was no reason why we should remain on the defensive.

The decision of the government was conveyed to the Eastern Navy Command and soon after this, a task force with Fleet Commander Rear Admiral A.K. Singh flying his flag on INS *Delhi*, sailed for the China Sea. It conducted joint exercises and manoeuvres with the Chinese Navy and even weathered Typhoon Saomai during this extended sortie in the mid-China Sea. Finally, in the end of September 2000, this Eastern Fleet Task Force entered the port of Shanghai and was accorded a grand ceremonial reception with Navy-style gun salutes exchanged and guards of honour paraded.

Well before this task force returned to its home base at Vishakhapatnam, reports from the Indian embassy in Beijing arrived with a glowing account of this event. It had been widely covered by not only China's national television network but the Western media had much to say about it as well.

For the Indian Navy, this came as no surprise and is perhaps best summed up by a military acronym—SOP, Standard Operating Procedure.

Since Navies worldwide operate in international waters, they have a professional understanding among themselves. But while Navies are conscious of their role and potential, it is the diplomats on either side of the border who really need to get attuned to the concept of naval operations.

Understanding Chinese strategic culture has never been easy but more often than not, it is our own geostrategic perceptions about China which are flawed. This is largely because our blinkered view that land is of utmost importance when it comes to defence has given us a 'continental' mindset that only seems to consider China as a landward neighbour.

Prime Minister Vajpayee had an open mind and could comprehend the strategic advantage that India's maritime dimension had to offer. This enabled him to approach the issue by dealing with China on equal terms. It was quite unlike the mortifying manner in which we have always been kowtowing to China. In contrast, it was Vajpayee who was never on the back foot.

CHAPTER 6

PARLIAMENT TERROR ATTACK AND OPERATION PARAKRAM

In a democracy, there may come a time when the Prime Minister finds it necessary to take a decision that is politically expedient but technically flawed—even from a military point of view.

This is perhaps why Operation Parakram, which had been conceived by the armed forces for an entirely different purpose went the way it did, after the terror attack on the Parliament of India. But all that is now history. It happened almost two decades ago, in December 2001.

I was then the Chairman of the tri-services Chiefs of Staff Committee (COSC) and concurrently, the Chief of the Indian Navy. My two colleagues were General Padmanabhan, the Army Chief and Air Chief Marshal Tipnis, the Air Force Chief.

•

Operation Parakram had been conceived in mid-2000 by the service Chiefs and meant to be a punishing response in the event of a Kargil type of misadventure by Pakistan. It was planned as a deep-penetration slicing blow by Indian Army formations in a designated sector and the unit commanders had been adequately briefed.

The convoluted form that Operation Parakram finally took became a subject of considerable introspection. It had been overtaken by events that had not really been foreseen, for what happened was not just a Kargil type of Pakistani misadventure, but a far more heinous attack than could ever be imagined.

On 13 December 2001, the Indian Parliament building in the heart of Delhi was attacked in broad daylight. Perpetrated by Pakistani Army-sponsored terror groups, this audacious attack on the very citadel of Indian democracy shocked and infuriated the nation and the mood was for immediate retaliation. Seven people were killed as well as the five terrorists who tried to enter the building.

Soon after this terror attack took place, the three armed forces' Chiefs hurriedly met with Defence Minister George Fernandes and National Security Advisor Brajesh Mishra in the Army operations room.

Discussions were focused on delivering a swift riposte which was the need of the hour and the contingency plan selected was to destroy a huge Pakistani army training camp for terrorists located across the LoC and deep inside Pakistan Occupied Kashmir (POK). With our Army units in full readiness and all systems in operation, a last-minute intelligence report caused a huge hiccup. Apparently, the Pakistani Army terror camp which was to be targeted had been cleverly relocated to a nearby site, sandwiched between a school and a large hospital.

Frantic consultations took place and the final decision of Prime Minister Vajpayee was to stand down. Accordingly, this operation was aborted, as striking the selected target would have resulted in unacceptable collateral damage. Shortly after the operation for a swift riposte had to be shelved, the three military Chiefs were summoned to the Prime Minister's residence. The senior cabinet ministers and the NSA were already in a close huddle with the Prime Minister. By the time we reached 7 Race Course Road, the cabinet had already taken its decision and the armed forces' Chiefs were directed to mobilise the armed forces for action. However, we were told that the mobilisation was not going to be for Operation Parakram as originally conceived and further instructions would follow.

Late that night, General Padmanabhan and I were informed by NSA Brajesh Mishra that the Prime Minister would have a private meeting with us over breakfast the next morning.

We had no inkling of what to expect, but during the breakfast meeting it became apparent that Prime Minister Vajpayee was viewing the mobilisation of the three armed forces purely as a coercive strategy and nothing more. Since it had been a rushed decision, the Prime Minister may have only later realised that the full-scale mobilisation which had been ordered could have serious implications for the armed forces.

This was my third year with Prime Minister Vajpayee and ever since the days of the Kargil war, when he had institutionalised his private meetings with the armed forces' Chiefs, one could sometimes discern his anxieties. Hence the raison d'être for this breakfast meeting may have been just that.

Since the Prime Minister was always a patient listener, the Army Chief and I used the opportunity to discreetly convey our misgivings about full-scale mobilisation of the armed forces and how the war wastage and massive effort involved could seriously degrade the long-term capability of the forces. But there are aspects of military operations that are not easy to explain in titbits, and from his distant gaze, we realised that Prime Minister Vajpayee had many matters on his mind and complex issues that urgently needed to be addressed. Apart from the hearty breakfast, the private interaction with the Prime Minister was as always, a great stress-buster.

We three Chiefs later met up with the Defence Minister. He had practically nothing to say at all and vaguely talked of 'coercive diplomacy' as the new avatar of the original Operation Parakram. Although the armed forces were alerted and ready for war with a distinct military edge over Pakistan, the directive to launch the operation never came—with the forces kept waiting from January to October 2002.

The terror attack on the Parliament of India will remain a milestone in our chequered past and for scholars of military history, Operation Parakram will always be an unresolved debate. It may have been politically expedient but from a military point of view, Operation Parakram was not its finest hour. It led to a massive dislocation of the armed forces' personnel and infrastructure with unjustified wastage of combat resources since the conflict did not take place—all of this without any clear military aim or objective.

CHAPTER 7

OPERATION ENDURING FREEDOM

Shortly after the 9/11 terror attacks in the US in 2001, high-level delegations arrived in India. They had come with a special request from the US President.

As the Chairman of the Chiefs of Staff Committee (COSC), I was required to interact with the military delegation and informed that their mission was highly classified—only after they arrived, would details be explained by them in person.

•

UNCLE SAM'S MESSAGE

Admiral Dennis Blair, the Commander-in-Chief of the US Pacific Command (now renamed the Indo-Pacific Command) was the leader of the military delegation. I had met Admiral Blair earlier on a few occasions, usually during the annual Indo-US Joint Exercise, 'Malabar'.

I was completely taken aback by the size of Admiral Blair's entourage. In tow with him were several high-ranking US military officers representing the Army, Navy, Air Force, and also the US Marine Corps. My office staff had been equally surprised but discreetly went about arranging for additional chairs and the extra *chai-pani ka bandobast* (refreshments).

In that brief moment before formal discussions commenced, Admiral Blair took me aside and quietly mentioned that this military delegation had been personally deputed by the US President, on the advice of General Harry Shelton, Chairman of the Joint Chiefs, who was my counterpart in the US. Admiral Blair added that the US government was keen on India's support for its war on terror and that a separate delegation headed by the former US Deputy Secretary of State, Strobe Talbot, was in dialogue with top Indian officials, including Foreign Minister Jaswant Singh and NSA Brajesh Mishra.

OPERATION ENDURING FREEDOM

The delegation had come well prepared and the PowerPoint presentation unveiled a US plan to attack Afghanistan and decimate the Al Qaeda and Taliban.

The codename for this operation was 'Enduring Freedom' and the assault was mainly to be launched from seaward by US naval forces operating in the North Arabian Sea, supported by long-range aircraft operating from air bases in the Indian Ocean.

The presentation was quite long-drawn-out, mainly to justify the launching of a global war on terror. Fortunately,

I was spared the tactical details of Operation Enduring Freedom as Admiral Dennis Blair was aware that I was quite familiar with the US concept of operations—the reason being that I had undergone advanced training in amphibious warfare with the US Navy.

Finally, the presentation led on to India's military participation in the US war on terror and it was here that the penny finally dropped. We realised that the delegation was proposing that the Indian armed forces join the US-led coalition for Operation Enduring Freedom, the war against Afghanistan. But the devil lay in the details, which precisely specified the tasks for the Indian armed forces.

ROLE OF THE INDIAN ARMED FORCES

The Indian Navy was to have a major involvement, since the inter-operability between the two Navies had been refined over the years, with regular joint exercises, such as 'Malabar'.

During the combat phase of Operation Enduring Freedom, the tasks for the Indian Navy included underway replenishment at sea and other combat related support for the US carrier battle groups. The IAF was to make its air bases available for staging-through of long-range US aircraft, while the Indian Army was to prepare to induct troops into Afghanistan for ground operations, after the assault from seaward was completed.

The presentation made by Admiral Blair and his team had me worried. I urgently needed to discuss this matter with my colleagues, the Army and Air Chiefs.

The US request had serious implications. My head was swirling after that two-hour-long briefing and I almost felt I was in quicksand.

•

CHIEFS STAND TOGETHER

There was complete unanimity between General Padmanabhan, Air Chief Marshal Tipnis, and I. We decided that our advice to the Cabinet Committee on Security would be as follows:

We ought not to get involved in Operation Enduring Freedom. Neither was this a United Nations operation, nor was India at war with Afghanistan. Moreover, with its policy of non-alignment, India had never been part of a military pact or alliance. India had for decades been involved in UN peacekeeping operations, but that has a moral dimension to it.

SHARPLY DIVIDED CCS

It was late that very same evening when the Cabinet Committee on Security met at the Prime Minister's residence and in attendance was only a select group, comprising a few senior cabinet ministers, the NSA, and the three armed forces' Chiefs.

The format for such meetings (since the Kargil war) had been standardised: the Chiefs were seated directly opposite the Prime Minister, facing him, and he was flanked by his cabinet ministers and the NSA. After Prime Minister Vajpayee was seated, he glanced at NSA Brajesh Mishra on his left, which was his cue to begin the discussion. Brajesh Mishra accordingly explained the request which had come from the President of the US for India to support the global war on terror and their plan to destroy the Al Qaeda and Taliban network inside Afghanistan.

Foreign Minister Jaswant Singh then took over and since he had a military background, he was able to provide operational details of the support being sought from our armed forces for Operation Enduring Freedom. He then waxed eloquent on the need to join this operation as it was part of a global war on terror and could garner international support, and so on. The Foreign Minister also mentioned his meeting with Strobe Talbot and his team of diplomats and the opportunity India had to engage with the US, the *only* superpower.

Prime Minister Vajpayee was an extremely observant person and must have noticed my look of disapproval as he remarked, '*Hamare Admiral khush nahi hai*' (our Admiral is not happy).

This gave me a chance to express the opinion of the Chiefs and I politely pointed out that Operation Enduring Freedom may have a noble objective but the Indian armed forces had never been part of any military alliance as non-alignment had always been India's foreign policy.

I could see that Foreign Minister Jaswant Singh was chomping at the bit, probably because I had strayed onto his turf. So I tactfully put in a query, 'Sir, if the Indian military is seen as part of the US attack on Afghanistan, would it not appear that India was at war with Afghanistan?'

General Padmanabhan joined the issue at this stage, expressing strong misgivings about Indian troops being inducted into Afghanistan when it wasn't even a UN operation. Air Chief Marshal Tipnis then promptly chipped in and mentioned that allowing our air bases and other military facilities to be used for Operation Enduring Freedom could set a wrong precedent.

There was an uneasy silence and the Prime Minister finally looked at Defence Minister George Fernandes, whose response was a one-liner: 'Our military chiefs have said it all.'

THE PRIME MINISTER'S INTERVENTION

The Prime Minister had soon realised that there were sharply divided views. But he had also clearly understood that there could be serious implications of committing the Indian armed forces for Operation Enduring Freedom. It could well turn out to be a bed of nails. So Prime Minister Vajpayee graciously put the matter to rest with a philosophical quip: '*Isko thoda aur sochna padega*' (This may need more thought).

And so it was how the matter was quietly buried and the US proposal for Operation Enduring Freedom never saw the light of day.

(L to R) General S. Padmanabhan, the author and Air Chief Marshal Anil Tipnis. The author was the Chairman of Chiefs of Staff Committee during Operation Enduring Freedom 2001.

Admiral Sushil Kumar assumes charge as Chairman of the Chiefs of Staff Committee (COSC) from outgoing Army Chief General Ved Malik on 30 September 2000.

CHAPTER 8

HIJACKING OF IC 814: *A FIVE-DAY ORDEAL*

The hijacking of Indian Airlines flight IC 814 and the hostage crisis that ensued thereafter, has been comprehensively documented in publications that range from riveting first-hand experiences to investigation reports and detailed analyses. Apart from the missed opportunity for armed personnel to storm into the plane during the hijacking phase when it landed in Amritsar for refuelling, even the wherewithal for handling the hostage crisis on the ground was woefully lacking.

One wonders what must have gone on in the mind of Prime Minister Vajpayee, who had to decide the fate of a plane load of Indians held hostage by hijackers thousands of kilometres away at Kandahar, in Taliban-controlled Afghanistan.

•

On 24 December 1999, an Indian Airlines Airbus 300 designated as IC 814 from Kathmandu in Nepal to the Delhi international airport, was hijacked when it entered Indian air space. The hijackers demanded that the aircraft be taken to Kandahar in Afghanistan via Dubai, but the plane was short on fuel and an unplanned landing at Amritsar became necessary. Despite the best efforts of the captain who was playing for time on ground, knowing it was the only chance for a rescue, the Crisis Management Group (CMG) under the Cabinet Secretary bungled the intervention plans. The frenzied hijackers quickly got suspicious and forced the pilot to take off at gunpoint.

The plane refuelled at Lahore in Pakistan and finally landed at Kandahar which at that time was almost entirely controlled by the Taliban. Since 27 out of the 176 passengers on board had been released en route at Dubai, the flight crew and the remaining passengers were held as hostages at Kandahar. The hijackers demanded the release of five hardcore terrorists imprisoned in India, one of whom was the recalcitrant Masood Azhar of the Jaish-e-Mohammed (JeM). He recently struck back at India by masterminding the massacre of more than 40 soldiers of the Central Reserve Police Force at Pulwama in Jammu and Kashmir on 13 February 2019.

HIJACKERS' DEMAND, NON-NEGOTIABLE

The hijack-cum-hostage crisis lasted for more than five days from Christmas Eve in December 1999 until the start of the new millennium and in the process one person was stabbed to death and 17 others brutally injured. Swapping the five Pakistani terrorists for the entire plane load of Indian citizens was the uncompromising demand of the Taliban hijackers, their ruthless intentions being clearly demonstrated by their actions.

A long-range Israeli -style Entebbe operation was simply out of the question—we just did not have that sort of capability. The only chance for a short-range intervention was when the plane landed at Amritsar but the CMG could not get its act together with alacrity and let that opportunity slip away. Prime Minister Vajpayee and his cabinet were thus faced with absolutely no options with 31 December as the ultimatum given by the hijackers for the swap.

The three armed forces' Chiefs were required to be present for the Cabinet Committee on Security (CCS) meetings, which were held frequently as the hijackers' ultimatum approached. Reflecting on this incident, I recall the sight of the anxious relatives of the hostages who waited patiently, day and night, outside the Prime Minister's residence. With no options left, I wondered what may have gone on in the mind of Prime Minister Vajpayee during that ordeal lasting for five long days.

PRIME MINISTER'S CALL

Came the day of the ultimatum and the CCS had to take a decision. The cabinet was sharply divided. The Prime Minister along with NSA Brajesh Mishra and Foreign Minister Jaswant Singh were in favour of swapping the hostages for the five terrorists, while the Deputy Prime Minister L.K. Advani and some others felt otherwise.

The buck finally stopped with Prime Minister Vajpayee and he made the important decision—the swap would be done.

Delegated with this responsibility by the Prime Minister, Foreign Minister Jaswant Singh accompanied the five terrorists in a special aircraft to Kandahar and brought back the Indians who had been held hostage by the Taliban for five days.

What may have been the consequences if Prime Minister Vajpayee had rejected the hijackers' ultimatum will forever remain in the realm of conjecture as well as many unanswered questions.

The hijacking of IC 814 brought in a new dimension to our travails with terror and the situation has steadily worsened. Hopefully, the wherewithal to handle such a crisis is today far better than it was two decades ago in 1999.

CHAPTER 9

ATTENTION, ALL HANDS!: PRIME MINISTER ON BOARD

In early 1999, the Indian Navy's latest warship, INS Mysore, *was to be inducted into service and Prime Minister Vajpayee had agreed to commission this state-of-the-art warship of the Indian Navy.*

•

One day, after a meeting of the Cabinet Committee on Security, I showed Prime Minister Vajpayee a photograph of the ship that he would be commissioning a couple of months later. Impressed by this formidable-looking guided missile destroyer, the Prime Minister casually remarked, 'I've never seen our Navy in action.'

'Take that as a hint,' whispered Defence Minister George Fernandes to me. Well, I did—there and then I tied up details with NSA Brajesh Mishra, who was also present.

The business of the Navy is at sea and so, having alerted Admiral Madhvendra Singh, the Commander-in-Chief Western

Naval Command, preparations began in full swing for the Prime Minister's visit to the Western Fleet.

ON BOARD THE FLAGSHIP

Embarked on board the aircraft carrier INS *Viraat*, the Prime Minister spent three days with the Western Fleet, the 'sword arm' of the Indian Navy. It was a tightly packed schedule in order to demonstrate the three-dimensional capability of our Navy.

CURIOSITY AT SEA

Every evening, while the Prime Minister was unwinding in his cabin, Admiral Madhvendra Singh and I would spend a while chit-chatting with him about the Navy's age-old customs and traditions. This seemed to greatly fascinate Vajpayeeji.

Regarding the Navy's latest warship, INS *Mysore*, yet to be commissioned, Vajpayeeji one day asked an interesting question about the naming of Navy warships. He asked, 'Why are Navy warships always given the same name as their decommissioned predecessors?' I gave him every possible explanation that included folklore and age-old traditions and practices in most Navies of the world and showed him an album with a photograph of the decommissioned *Mysore* of World War II vintage and the state-of-the-art INS *Mysore* that he would be commissioning. The Prime Minister appeared thoughtful and distracted and I could sense that something was bothering him.

Next morning just before the combat demonstrations commenced, I casually asked Defence Minister George Fernandes if there was something on the Prime Minister's mind. It was only then that the mystery was revealed. It had all to do with two new warships that were slated to be commissioned into the Indian Navy as INS *Bombay* and INS *Calcutta*.

The immediate problem concerned the next warship that was to be commissioned as INS *Bombay* and was similar to the other guided missile destroyers of the same class—INS *Delhi* and INS *Mysore*. In accordance with Navy tradition, both ships had been named after major cities of India and were given the same names as their predecessors, which had since been decommissioned. Since HMIS *Bombay* had been a decommissioned sloop in days gone by, INS *Bombay* had been accepted as the name for the newest warship. (Before 1947, Indian Navy warship names had the prefix 'HMIS' [Her Majesty's Indian Ship] as they belonged to the British Royal Navy and were jointly manned by both British and Indian Navy officers and sailors).

Navy warships take years to build before they are commissioned into active service and therefore, deciding the name of a new warship is invariably done well in advance. Accordingly, since the government had already approved the ship's name as INS *Bombay*, a sudden glitch had arisen as the city of Bombay had been renamed subsequently and given its pre-colonial 'vernacular' name of Mumbai.

It would have been a different matter if INS *Bombay* had already been commissioned into active service before the city of Bombay was renamed Mumbai. But to commission a new warship with *Bombay* as its name when the city's name had already been changed to Mumbai did present a serious anomaly.

'The old order changeth, yielding place to new...' were the wise words of King Arthur in Lord Alfred Tennyson's poem and four centuries ago, while referring quite specifically to names, it was William Shakespeare who proclaimed: '*What's in a name? That which we call a rose by any other name would smell as sweet*'.

PRIME MINISTER VAJPAYEE BELLS THE CAT

It was a tricky situation with the ball being squarely in the court of Prime Minister Vajpayee as the head of the government. And I vividly recall Prime Minister Vajpayee's pensive words that conveyed his thoughts: 'India has a great historical past with traditions that are also ingrained in our armed forces. That is why our nation should never forget its past.'

These words reflected Vajpayeeji's infinite wisdom, which also conveyed his decision: So, rightly did it happen that INS *Bombay* was commissioned as INS *Mumbai* and INS *Calcutta* was commissioned as INS *Kolkata*.

Prime Minister Vajpayee meets the Navy's fighter pilots on the flight deck of INS *Viraat*. The author is on extreme right, wearing a beret.

The Prime Minister spent three days at sea on board the aircraft carrier INS *Viraat*.

in accordance with Clause III of the United Nations Convention on the Law of the Sea (UNCLOS). The directive to 'Proceed with dispatch to intercept the suspicious ship' would have been interpreted by the Indian Navy's task force Commander as prescribed in the Standard Operating Procedure (SOP): 'Go at full speed to inspect and verify the credentials of a suspicious ship masquerading as *Mega Rama* and apprehend (capture) this vessel, using force, if necessary.' (UNCLOS empowers all Navies to act in this way to curb piracy and terrorism at sea.)

A task force of the Western Fleet, which was on a routine patrol near the Gulf led by a Delhi class missile destroyer, was accordingly diverted to intercept the suspicious ship and directed to proceed with despatch but await final orders for interception. Meanwhile, frantic discussions were on, between the MoD and the MEA and the ball had finally landed up in the court of Foreign Minister Jaswant Singh.

ACQUAINTANCES OF YORE

In the mid-1950s, Foreign Minister Jaswant Singh and I were both young cadets, training to be officers at the National Defence Academy. Both of us were very keen horsemen and fond of polo. With his superb equestrian talent, Jaswant Singh was easily inducted by the Indian Army as a cavalry officer, while I found myself riding the waves at sea!

More than four decades later, destiny brought us together at the national capital in Delhi and we renewed our passion for horse riding and polo. It was at one of our daily equestrian outings that the topic of *Alondra Rainbow* cropped up. Since the Japanese ambassador had already met Foreign Minister Jaswant Singh, I only needed to fill in the blanks.

Operation Alondra Rainbow began as a routine interception at sea but within a few hours the situation had acquired serious international implications. With the suspicious ship racing towards the coastal waters of Saudi Arabia, a hot pursuit would require approval at the highest governmental level. Foreign Minister Jaswant Singh advised us to seek the opinion of Prime Minister Vajpayee.

VAJPAYEE'S DECISION

Prime Minister Vajpayee had been suitably briefed in advance about the fast-paced developments at sea and the serious implications of intercepting a foreign ship mid-ocean, which could have unforeseen international repercussions.

The meeting with the Prime Minister lasted for barely a few minutes and it was Foreign Minister Jaswant Singh who did all the talking and explaining in his eloquent style and baritone voice. Defence Minister Fernandes and I were silent spectators.

Finally, giving his usual characteristic nod, the Prime Minister, said, 'If you have no doubts, complete your mission.'

A SUCCESSFUL OPERATION

With the green signal from the Prime Minister, the task force Commander at sea was given the go ahead to intercept the suspicious vessel masquerading as *Mega Rama*. By late afternoon, signals from the Western Fleet confirmed that *Mega Rama* had been successfully intercepted almost 800 kilometres from the Indian coast.

As the Indian Navy's task force encircled the vessel, the pirates on board panicked. Nabbed red-handed, the desperadoes tried to frantically destroy all evidence by pulling out the plugs in the vessel and scuttling their ship. But swift intervention by the Indian Navy task force foiled their attempts.

Finally in utter panic, the pirates triggered off the emergency satellite-linked distress alarm, not realising that the first part of the pre-coded radio message would be the name of the ship—and *Alondra Rainbow* it indeed was! Marine Commandos from the Indian Navy warships immediately slithered down from helicopters and swiftly rounded up the pirates.

That evening I had a surprise visitor at my office. It was the Japanese ambassador. He was excited and ecstatic about the Indian Navy's action in rescuing *Alondra Rainbow*. Frankly, till that moment I had not realised the significance of this event and what a boost it had given to Indo-Japanese relations and to international maritime cooperation in general.

For the Indian Navy and Coast Guard, it was just another operation in the normal course of duty but the acclaim that the nation received was an immense reward in itself. Seen in hindsight, the Alondra Rainbow incident turned out to be a riveting mid-ocean operation that brought our nation international acclaim from the maritime community.

Yet, how many would know that none of this would have been possible but for the split-second decision of Prime Minister Vajpayee, who gave the green signal to the Navy. The trust and confidence that he reposed in his team was inspirational but more than that was his ability to take extremely difficult decisions in matters that could have serious international repercussions.

Prime Minister Vajpayee never had the benefit of hindsight as we have today, two decades later. But he certainly had remarkable foresight that enabled him to take such a weighty decision—in real time.

Operation Alondra Rainbow was a mid-ocean interception of a pirated vessel by an Indian Navy task force in 1999.
Photo courtesy: Indian Navy Archive

An Indian Navy task force, led by a Delhi Class Guided Missile Destroyer, was diverted with full despatch for Operation Alondra Rainbow.

CHAPTER 11

IN A LIGHTER VEIN

HUMOUR AT SEA

There was a lighter side to Prime Minister Vajpayee that I discovered when he embarked on board our aircraft carrier INS *Viraat* in the spring of 1999. He spent an unforgettable three days at sea with our Western Fleet. The Indian Navy was certainly honoured to have him on board. He seemed fascinated by this experience though it must have been a hectic schedule with never a dull moment.

Every evening, while he was relaxing in his cabin, Admiral Madhvendra Singh and I would give him some company. Quite

A newspaper clipping (courtesy Times of India dated 5 December 2000) read: 'Prime Minister Atal Bihari Vajpayee steering Navy Chief Admiral Sushil Kumar in the right direction at a reception on Navy Day on Monday.'

apart from being thrilled by the combat demonstration provided by the fleet, he seemed enthralled by life at sea and enjoyed the real life stories we often related to him during these informal sessions.

Finally, the moment came for his departure. In accordance with tradition, I formally presented him the Indian Navy's crest and requested him to sign the visitors' book and pen down his remarks. Specially procured and embossed with the Western Fleet emblem, the visitors' book's first page bore the boldly printed words: 'Message of the Prime Minister'. The Prime Minister looked at me thoughtfully so I discreetly interjected, 'Sir, even a one-liner would be fine.'

When it was done, I jokingly told him about Prime Minister Rajiv Gandhi's remark in the visitors' book of our nuclear submarine INS *Chakra*: 'Thank God I was a pilot—not a Navy submariner.'

Prime Minister Vajpayees's quip was spontaneous: 'I wish I could say I'm better off as a politician!'

And that's just one example of his sense of humour.

THE IMPORTANCE OF BEING 'DAS'

In 1960, our batch of midshipmen was on board the flagship INS *Mysore* for a one-year training stint. The senior batch before us had completed training on INS *Mysore* and had joined their fleet ships after being commissioned as Sub-lieutenants.

One Sunday morning, when INS *Mysore* was anchored in the Bombay (now Mumbai) harbour, an announcement was relayed from the ship's broadcast system: 'Telephone call for Midshipman Das.'

Surprised though he was, Midshipman Das, popularly known as Davy alias *Chotu*, wasted no time and sprinted to the Wireless Office. When Davy returned looking ashen-faced and nervous, we were perturbed that the call must have been about bad news, so we gently made discreet inquiries. Suddenly he blurted out in anguish, 'It was a girl, damn it! But I don't even know who she was!'

We grilled Davy Das for possible clues and it soon transpired that it was a case of mistaken identity. The girl had obviously called to re-establish contact with a Midshipman Das of the previous batch and that could only have been Midshipman Premvir Das who had left INS *Mysore* long ago. On second thoughts, this shore call could well be the chance of a lifetime. Being new to Bombay, we were woefully short of company on the female front. So our think tank got into the act, puzzling over how to establish contact with the unknown girl. This was a huge hurdle. Who was she? Where was she? How to find her? This sleuth operation would require the genius of a Sherlock Holmes!

Finally, the titbits of information were pieced together and it turned out that the rendezvous would have to be at 8 p.m. near Flora Fountain outside the Khatau Voiles shop where this girl and her friends were working. The plot was hatched and the selected team comprised the six-foot-three-inch Aku Roy who was built like a bear and would come in handy in case there was close combat, Slim Verma, and I, since I was part of Davy's inner circle.

The only thing that bothered us was that the girl and her friends would be expecting the smart and debonair Premvir Das, not a bunch of ruffians. But all's well that ends well—contact was established without any fiasco. And from then on, for us hard-up bachelors, there was no looking back.

Even William Shakespeare got it wrong when he wrote: 'What's in a name?'

COOKING UP TROUBLE

As a young Lieutenant, I was commanding a small patrol vessel with just four officers and two dozen sailors on board. The kitchen, known in Navy parlance as the 'galley', was common for all ranks on board and food was laid out in buffet-style, with self-service as the norm. Being the Captain of the vessel, I had the privilege of being served in my cabin.

Aware of my personal food preferences, the ship's cook sometimes inflicted these preparations on the entire ship's crew. One day I heard a commotion break loose in the ship's galley and when I asked what had happened, I was informed that a few dissatisfied chaps had roundly abused the cook.

The culprits could not be traced but according to the galley rumour, several expletives had been hurled at the poor cook. The one that particularly hurt his sentiments was *Suwwar ka baccha*, which literally translates to 'Son of a pig.'

In accordance with navy practice, I immediately ordered 'All lower decks to be cleared' and all hands to be lined up on the upper deck for the Captain's address. After reprimanding all of them suitably, I cooled off and announced that I would be willing to overlook this folly if the culprits would immediately apologise for calling the cook a *Suwwar ka baccha*.

There was a soft murmur at the rear and then a squeaky voice was heard saying, 'Sir, we are very sorry for calling him that, but can someone please tell us who called this *Suwwar ka baccha* a cook!'

FAUX PAS AT SEA

The fleet had sailed for a day at sea with Members of Parliament on board. The ship I was commanding was INS *Amini*, an anti-submarine corvette powered by gas turbines. Since it was my first sortie with Admiral Subimal Mookerjee, the Fleet Commander, I was keen to impress him.

I got my opportunity when the screen around the aircraft carrier was reoriented to simulate a new threat scenario. With gas turbines at full throttle, INS *Amini* raced across to her new screening station, sharply whizzing past the flagship. I thought it was a masterly manoeuvre and would surely impress the Admiral and the MPs.

I was pleased with myself when the Signal Communications Officer (SCO) shouted, 'Sir, signal from flagship!' Mentally prepared for the approving 'Bravo Zulu' from the Admiral, I puffed up my chest and said, 'Very well, read it out.'

In a loud voice, the SCO read out the signal from the Admiral: 'Your manoeuvre was foolhardy—NEGAT "Bravo Zulu".'

I noticed that one of the MPs was curiously peering over my shoulder. Mustering my wits, I quickly responded, 'Very good. Tell the Crypto Office to decode the signal!'

ALL IN GOOD TIME

In the spring of 1985, a squadron of anti-submarine ships that I was commanding had arrived on a visit to Kota Kinabalu in East Malaysia, which was a great equestrian and polo centre. So I was delighted when I got the opportunity to play a special polo match for the Governor's team. His Excellency was also present as the guest of honour.

After the match, the Governor was in very good humour as his team had won and he casually asked if he could visit our ships en route to his palace. My pulse raced as I wondered what the protocol would be to receive such a high-ranking foreign dignitary. Hoping there would be no faux pas, we alerted the ships and frantic efforts were made to welcome His Excellency, the Governor of East Malaysia. Unfortunately, the regular team that comprised the ceremonial guard of honour had gone ashore, so a new team had to be hastily assembled and briefed for this special occasion.

The Governor was in a joyous mood and enjoyed the fanfare, not noticing the sloppy drill movements of the ceremonial guard. But I surely did. Glaring at the young guard officer, I snarled at him, 'You must have good timing.'

About an hour later, the duty officer at the gangway was informed that the Governor was ready to leave and instructed to ensure a smart performance by the guard of honour. In utter panic, the duty officer reported that the ceremonial guard had dispersed as apparently, I had told them to do so. Baffled about what the conceivable reason for the dispersal could have been, a frantic search was begun and a new guard of honour press-ganged for the occasion. Thankfully, His Excellency was having a jolly time on board and was in no hurry to leave.

When it was all over and done with, I summoned the Guard Officer and demanded an explanation for the guard of honour's dispersal. In reply, he stammered, 'B...b...ut sir, you were the one who told us to have a good time.'

Stumped and speechless, I fumbled for a befitting reprimand, but the humour of the situation struck me—all said and done, English is a foreign language for us Indians and even the Governor had a good time!

HIGH AND DRY

My wife Venita had been a landlubber before we got married and in 1989, she was thrilled when we arrived in Bombay. As the Flag Officer Commanding Maharashtra (FOMA), I was allotted a heritage bungalow as our residence, called FOMA House. It was by the sea, at the southernmost tip of Bombay.

Adding to the bungalow's quaint ambience and spectacular location was a majestic old lighthouse— Prong's Reef Lighthouse—barely 400 metres from FOMA House. And when the tide flowed out, this tall lighthouse was approachable from FOMA House on foot since the reef became absolutely dry, the tidal range in Mumbai being about 12 feet. It certainly was a tantalizing sight and Venita had often toyed with the idea of dashing across this rocky and slippery reef to the lighthouse.

One day, while I was at sea for flotilla exercises, our ship received a strange message from the Harbour Control: 'Admiral's wife rescued from Prong's Reef Lighthouse. All OK.'

I was board INS *Sukanya* and Captain Rusi Contractor who was there too looked worried. But I knew what had possibly happened.

When I reached FOMA House, Venita was in ecstasy and recounted her escapade, walking across the reef to the lighthouse, having tea and snacks with the lighthouse keepers, and how Indian Navy MARCOS (Marine Commandos) deployed at the Bombay harbour waterfront noticed where she was and finally escorted her back to FOMA House.

I then remembered an old saying: 'You can lead a horse to water but you can't make it drink.' She had done exactly what she'd longed to do, regardless of the peril she could have faced!

'The time has come,' the Walrus said,
'to talk of many things:
of shoes and ships – and sealing wax
– of cabbages and Kings.'

Lewis Carroll, Alice's Adventures in Wonderland & Through the Looking-Glass

PART II

LOOKING BACK

CHAPTER 12

IF WISHES WERE HORSES...

'I joined the Navy to see the world ...' *were the lyrics of a popular song when I was a school boy in the early 1950s and for landlubbers like me who had never seen the sea, the Navy seemed a fascinating career. Added to that, my grandfather, who spent many years of his life in Singapore, had stirred my imagination with exciting tales of oceanic voyages and adventure.*

My eldest brother, Vijay, was a brilliant scholar who chose the medical profession and finally settled down abroad. Later, when my elder brother, Sudhir, whom I idolised for his amazing sporting talent, joined the National Defence Academy (NDA) as a Navy cadet, I could think of nothing better to do and promptly followed suit.

•

IMPRESSIONABLE DAYS

As a young impressionable teenager in the mid-1950s, I found myself training to be an officer at India's most prestigious tri-services' military training establishment—the National Defence Academy.

The author receiving 'Spurs' for outstanding horsemanship at NDA from the then Army Chief, General Thimayya.

What impressed me most was the sprawling campus of the NDA located on the Deccan plateau in the outskirts of Pune in a suburb known as Khadakwasla. The training facilities that were provided for young potential officers of the Army, Navy and Air Force were truly awesome. From mountain climbing to horse riding to sailing and flying—all the facilities were there. And there was even a polo ground! This was much more than I had ever expected.

Excited though I was at the thought of sailing on the high seas, I soon realised that my heart was actually elsewhere. It was the equestrian world of horses and polo that had always infatuated me and so the thought of joining the Army as a cavalry officer gradually crossed my mind. Confused though I was, the idea certainly sent my adrenalin flowing.

Since childhood, horse riding had been my great passion and I must say that I acquitted myself rather well in the sport. In my very first term at the NDA, I earned the coveted award of

'Spurs' for outstanding horsemanship, which was presented to me by the then Army Chief, General Thimayya .

Thereafter, I could only dream of a life in the cavalry and its poetic depiction in Tennyson's *Charge of the Light Brigade*. I was torn between two attractive options—the Navy, which had been my first choice and the Army, which had now become my heart's desire.

CHANGE OF TACK

As it happened, I caught the eye of the NDA Commandant, Major General Habibullah. Being an accomplished horseman himself, the Commandant was quick to spot my equestrian talent. This helped me to make up my mind and I readily opted to switch from the Navy to the Army.

I gathered, it would be just a routine procedure before formal approval was received from the services' headquarters at Delhi. And since it had the personal backing of the Commandant, it only seemed a matter of time. I was thrilled by this turn of events and conjured up grand visions of strutting around as a cavalry officer and serving in the elite 61st Cavalry Regiment of the Indian Army. It was an invigorating thought and I felt euphoric.

BACK TO SQUARE ONE

Aptly has it been said that *'Man proposes but God disposes'*, for shortly thereafter, General Habibullah left the NDA and a new

Commandant arrived on the scene. Strikingly handsome with stylish mannerisms, this Indian Navy Admiral certainly looked intimidating, at least from a distance.

In the hierarchy of the military, a cadet is perhaps the lowest form of life and so to me it hardly mattered who the Commandant was. At least so I thought, till I came face to face with the new Commandant—Admiral Benjamin Abraham Samson, affectionately known in the Navy as 'Chippy Samson'.

It was at a horse show held in honour of the new Commandant that I got the rare opportunity to meet Admiral Samson and it was only because I had performed a few impressive trick riding stunts that I got singled out for this introduction. As Admiral Samson shook my hand, I seemed to overhear someone whisper, *'I had originally joined the NDA as a Navy cadet but was now all set to join the cavalry'*. Somehow the remark did not register, at least that's what I thought.

When I was congratulated by the Commandant himself, I was all puffed up and euphoric. But alas, my high spirits were short-lived. I was summoned by my Divisional Officer, who grilled me in the true NDA boot camp style. All I can recall of the next day is that all hell broke loose!

Early next morning, I was 'lined-up' in the ceremonial drill order outside the Commandant's office for what is euphemistically termed as an 'interview'. For NDA cadets, it had many dreaded connotations. All that I was told was that it had something to do with my request to switch over from the Navy to the Army and join the 61st Cavalry.

I was trembling and dazed as I awaited my turn to be 'marched in' by the Subedar Major and from the corner of my

The author receiving the Polo trophy on behalf of the Navy team from Field Marshal Sam Manekshaw.

eye, I noticed my Squadron Commander Harish Bhagat seemed extremely nervous. His body language got me worried but mercifully my agony was over in a few seconds after sweating profusely, I was summoned into the office.

In his sparkling white uniform, Admiral Samson was standing ramrod straight in front of his desk and looked at me quizzically from top to toe. The interview was one-sided for I was tongue-tied.

'So you're fond of riding horses.'

'Sir.'

'Riding the waves is even better.'

'Sir.'

'And you chose the Navy...'

'Sir.'

'You chose right, so keep it that way.'

That was it. My interview lasted barely five seconds. And the Indian Navy thus became my career, my way of life.

That was December 1958.

Even though I served in the Indian Navy, my passion for horse riding and polo never faded and in 1969 we even put together a Navy polo team with Lieutenant Johnny Siga as the sheet anchor. I recall the time when the Indian Navy had won the prestigious Maharaja Prithi Singh Baria Polo Trophy and that too, by beating the much fancied 61st Cavalry team. Field Marshal Sam Manekshaw was the guest of honour and I still remember his witty remark as he handed me the trophy , *'If you sailors ran your ships as well as you ride horses, we would even have a fine Navy.'*

LOOKING BACK IN TIME

My initial career in the Navy took me to all parts of the globe which gave me an opportunity to interact with diverse armed forces. After an initial training attachment with the British Royal Navy in the Pacific, I was later selected for an advanced course in amphibious warfare in California in the US. But perhaps the most unique

The author as a Lieutenant on deputation to the British Royal Navy.

experience I had was training with the Warsaw Pact Navies in the Baltic Sea, while I was in command of an amphibious warfare ship that I commissioned in Poland at the height of the cold war in the mid-1970s.

My four decades of active duty with the Indian armed forces were a combination of challenging operational assignments which were interspersed with high-level appointments at the Integrated Headquarters of the Ministry of Defence (MoD). It was at the MoD that I had an opportunity to interact with the government as the

The author as Chief of the Indian Navy.

Director of Naval Operations (1988–90), Assistant Navy Chief (1992–94), Chief of Personnel (1996–97) and Vice Chief of the Navy (1996–97). Functioning in the corridors of power was an illuminating experience that provided me an insight into the relationship that existed between the governments of the day and the armed forces.

I graduated from the NDA, my alma mater, in 1958 and 40 years later, almost to the date, in December 1998, I was appointed in command of the Indian Navy as a four-star Admiral. It was at my tri-services alma mater that Commandant Admiral Chippy Samson had taken a decisive step that brought me to my senses from a world of luminous fantasy down to sea level.

Since the memory of that fateful interview at the NDA had not faded, among the first things I decided to do after my appointment was to pay my respects to Admiral Samson. Four decades is a long time and as I drove to Admiral Samson's residence at the Asian Games township, I wondered if he would even remember. But I was wrong. Long since retired and somewhat frail, Admiral Samson was staying with his daughter Leela Samson, a renowned exponent of Bharatnatyam, the Indian classical dance form.

We talked of many things and I recounted my days in the Navy after I left the NDA. Finally, placing his hand on my shoulder, he smiled as he said to me, 'Sushil, you may have made a better horseman than a sailor but I wonder if you would have risen beyond the rank of a Major in the Army's elite 61st Cavalry!'

Even with advancing age, Admiral Samson had not lost his sense of humour nor forgotten those memorable times at the NDA. It had been an unforgettable meeting and as I prepared to leave, he handed me an envelope, adding in jest, 'Read this in your spare time. Even Admirals sometimes need to laugh at themselves!'

In the envelope was a quote from George Bernard Shaw, on life in the Navy in the days of sailing, which went something like this:

'Men go to the Navy . . . thinking they will enjoy it. They do enjoy it for about a year, at least the stupid ones do, riding back and forth quite dully on their ships . . .

Gradually they become crazy. Crazier and crazier . . . Only the Navy has no way of distinguishing . . . between the sane and the insane . . .

If they are not mad before this, they go mad then. And the maddest of these become Admirals.

GEORGE BERNARD SHAW, 1884

CHAPTER 13

GLORY AT SEA: OPERATION CACTUS

Operation Cactus, India's military intervention at the request of then President Gayoom of the Maldives in 1988 was a spontaneous response that was swiftly executed. Operation Cactus had always been a tri-service contingency plan where the Navy's role was to provide a cordon sanitaire from seaward. But who would have ever imagined that a mission to thwart a coup in the island capital of Male would finally be accomplished more than a 1000 kilometres away and turn out to be a historic mid-ocean rescue operation.

When Operation Cactus was executed, I happened to be Director of Naval Operations (DNO) at the Indian Navy's operations centre in Delhi—and this is how it all happened.

•

After the Indian Air Force rapidly inducted an Indian Army parachute brigade at the airport on Hulule Island, adjacent to

Male, the rebel group who were Sri Lankan mercenaries of the People's Liberation Organization of Thamil Eelam (PLOTE) cadre, ran for cover and grabbing hostages from ashore, hijacked a merchant ship called *Progress Light*, which was anchored in the Male harbour.

With its motley group of seven hostages that included a Maldivian minister and his Swiss mother-in-law, the hijacked ship raced out of the Male harbour under the cover of darkness into the open waters of the Indian Ocean. But unknown to rebel leader Abdullah Luthufi on board *Progress Light*, the vessel was being shadowed by long-range maritime aircraft of the Indian Navy and a high speed Navy task force led by INS *Godavari*, with Captain Gopalachari in command, was fast closing in.

As the drama unfolded at sea, the Indian Navy operations room in Delhi was palpably tense yet privileged by the distinguished presence of then Prime Minister Rajiv Gandhi who was keenly following the action. The Maldivian President had personally requested that the rebels be captured and brought back to Male to face trial, so ensuring the safety of the hostages and also rounding up the rebels was certainly going to be a daunting task. This was evident from the incalculable difficulty of the mission flashed to Captain Gopalachari, the task force Commander at sea: '*Rescue the hostages and capture the rebels.*'

On board INS *Godavari*, the task force Commander prepared the warships under his command for an unusual Navy mission. It was going to be a mid-ocean hostage rescue operation and in preparation for this mission, special teams of MARCOS (Marine Commandos) had been lifted on helicopters and embarked on warships of this task force. Trained for special operations,

MARCOS of the Indian Navy have the versatile capability of being inserted into operations by air, surface, or underwater means. They provided the task force Commander with a handy asset for his mission.

When dawn broke on the following day, the rebels on *Progress Light* were startled by the menacing-looking warships of the Indian Navy task force that had stealthily encircled the hijacked ship during the night. Agitated and confused, the rebels refused to communicate with the force and pressed on doggedly in a north-easterly direction. Their intentions were clearly to seek refuge in Sri Lanka, as confirmed by radio transmissions monitored by Indian Navy warships.

A TRICKY OPERATION

After hours of inaction at sea, a terse message from the Sri Lankan Navy (SLN) came like a bombshell to the Indian Navy operations room: *'The SLN has been directed by its government to destroy the rebel ship if it approached within 100 miles of the Sri Lankan coast.'*

Our sources also confirmed that SLN gunboats had commenced their 'Sea and Action' drill and were manoeuvring out of the Colombo harbour. It was clear that the Sri Lankan ultimatum posed an operational dilemma for the Indian Navy, since the rebels were hell-bent on taking the ship to Sri Lanka. Moreover, the mandate given to the SLN could also provoke a naval confrontation which could have ruined everything.

With the rebel ship approaching the 100-mile limit stipulated by Sri Lanka, Operation Cactus had become a complex multinational situation. It now involved the Indian and Sri Lankan Navies, with hostages from the Maldives, including a Swiss national and also the rebel group who belonged to the terrorist outfit banned in Sri Lanka.

CAMARADERIE AT SEA

Fortunately, Navies worldwide have a professional understanding between themselves since they operate in a common medium and between the Indian Navy and the SLN, the relationship had always been amicable. So at this tense moment, Admiral Bunny Suri, my immediate boss at the operations centre, struck on a brilliant idea. He obtained the permission of Navy Chief Admiral 'Podgy' Nadkarni so that I could speak directly to my counterpart in the SLN, Commodore Clancy Fernando, DNO, SLN. I knew him well, as he had been my student at our Defence Services Staff College in the Nilgiris and we had remained in touch since then.

The hotline can be an extremely handy device and more so when the person at the other end happens to be a personal friend. So a rather tense situation was temporarily defused and gave the operations staff at Delhi a few minutes to carry out a snap appreciation of the changed operational situation.

IMMEDIATE AIM SIGNALLED

Concluding the operation swiftly had become an operational imperative so a flash signal was transmitted to the task force

Commander on board INS *Godavari*. It gave him an 'Immediate Aim': '*Stop Progress Light*.'

Since the situation at sea was best known to the task force's Commander who was at the scene of action, the flash signal from the Navy's operations centre at Delhi was unambiguous and left him in no doubt.

Captain Gopalachari rose to the occasion and superbly improvised on the art of coercive diplomacy. Using his linguistic skills in south Indian languages, he personally engaged Abdullah Luthufi, the rebel leader, in a bout of friendly negotiations, while the Indian Navy warships—*Godavari*, *Betwa*, and *Tir*—provided a convincing firepower demonstration, through a well-timed action sequence.

SITUATION REPORTS

SITREPS, which in Navy terms or format are Situation Reports, gave a precise account of this action at sea.

Four inch shells shattered the foremast, ack-ack fire raked the focsle deck, knocking out the anchors and then a massive undersea explosion from a depth charge dropped by a helicopter sent a spine-chilling shudder through the rebel ship, which brought *Progress Light* to a dead halt, lying motionless in the water. Before the dazed rebels realised what was happening, Navy commandos stormed on board and then it was all over.

'*Hostages Rescued Safely and Rebels Captured*.' This was the final message from Captain Gopalachari that brought down the curtain on Operation Cactus.

Merchant vessel *Progress Light* (hijacked by the rebels) being intercepted by Indian Navy warships in the Indian Ocean during Operation Cactus in November 1988. The Indian Navy task force was led by INS *Godavari*, which is seen in the foreground. Photo courtesy: Indian Navy Archive

Hostages rescued by the Indian Navy task force during Operation Cactus being ferried to the Navy warships. Among the rescued were a Maldivian Minister and his Swiss mother-in-law. Photo courtesy: Indian Navy Archive

INS *Godavari* Captain Srinivasa Varadachari Gopalachari with Abdullah Luthufi, the rebel leader, after he was captured by the Indian Navy at sea, during Operation Cactus. Photo courtesy: Indian Navy Archive

Abdullah Luthufi, the rebel leader, after he was captured by the Indian Navy during Operation Cactus. Photo courtesy: Indian Navy Archive

'Bravo Zulu', which is 'well done' in the Navy's signal format was the response from the operations centre at Delhi.

As the list of rescued hostages was displayed on the giant screen in the Navy operations room, Rajiv Gandhi remarked light-heartedly: 'I wonder if the Maldivian minister will forgive the Indian Navy for also rescuing his mother-in-law!'

Admiral Gopalachari (fondly known as Chari) served with great distinction and rose to be the Deputy Chief of the Indian Navy. He is no more, but will always be remembered for his role as the task force's Commander during Operation Cactus. It seemed a mission impossible but Chari made it happen and brought glory to the nation.

CHAPTER 14

DOWN BY THE SEA: FACING THE GROUND REALITY

Come December every year and Navy Day sends a flush of adrenalin through the Indian Navy. Proudly proclaiming its war-fighting role, the Silent Service, the stealthy submarines, justifies the need for a strong Navy. That has always been the standard Navy format. Yet, year in and year out, it seemed like a sad lament.

•

THE NAVY'S BLUES

Each year, marching down Rajpath on Republic Day, the Indian Navy contingent in their resplendent navy blue uniforms is indeed a rare sight but hopefully it reminds our citizens that we also have a Navy.

Deep within, the Indian Navy knows that it has to reckon with a nation besieged by a 'continental' outlook, which predicates the ground reality. And so the Navy of India, has remained the Cinderella among the armed forces.

CONTINENTAL OBSESSION

Even the most profound enlightenment about the fact that India is actually a maritime country with a maritime DNA, is overshadowed by problems that plague our land frontiers. With a security paradigm conditioned by an LOC orientation, it's not without reason that our focus remains riveted to the north and since the seas around the subcontinent seem calm and peaceful, the disturbed Himalayan borders compellingly draw our attention.

Our continental obsession is almost reminiscent of the Napoleonic mindset, when France's weakness lay exposed at sea despite the country's military dominance on land in Europe. Yet in this strange psychological milieu, historical evidence matters little. Who cares that the world was reshaped through naval power or that India was actually colonised from seaward by the superior naval forces of the British?

That may only be a footnote in our history. Yet from the days of the Roman empire, the maritime logic has been emphatic: *To be secure on land, one has to be strong at sea.*

I recall the time when Prime Minister Vajpayee spent a couple of days with our Western Fleet. The Navy's combat readiness was on display and the Prime Minister seemed pleased to see the business end of the Indian Navy. It was an opportune moment or so I felt, as I purposefully broached the need to strengthen the Navy's force levels. Even as he seemed to give me a profound nod, I noticed that his mind was preoccupied. It was April 1999 and a month later Kargil happened.

NUCLEAR OBSESSION

Apart from the nation's continental outlook, there is another problem that could derail the Indian Navy from its path of development. It concerns the nation's obsession with the nuclear arms race.

The strategic importance of the seaward leg of the nuclear triad can never be questioned and as long as the ocean medium remains impervious to the electro-magnetic spectrum, the ICBM-firing submarine will remain the ultimate deterrent. After years of painstaking in-house development, the Indian Navy has joined that exclusive league. It's an achievement that only a few advanced Navies of the world can boast of, yet it has also left the Indian Navy in a predicament.

CART BEFORE THE HORSE

Armed forces are meant for war and *war-fighting* is all about conventional combat capability, unless one foolishly believes that nuclear wars can be fought and won, especially so between neighbours, which would be sheer *hara-kiri*. Even the scheming Generals across the border realised the reality of this during Kargil.

Joining the ICBM league may have showcased our technological prowess but raises an important question—where do we go from here? Misconceived notions about fighting nuclear wars may belong to the realm of luminous fantasy but they still exist in certain quarters—even in our country. It would therefore, be prudent for the powers that be to take a hard look at our Agni intercontinental ballistic missile programme before it becomes an obsession in itself. Since the armed forces are hardly consulted on such matters and the military Chiefs discreetly kept out of the loop, one wonders who takes these lofty decisions.

Our nuclear warfare gurus have their own predilections and seem hell-bent on stockpiling a nuclear arsenal by using up scarce national resources, whereas the more compelling need has been to modernise our conventional war-fighting capability. Sadly, we seem to have placed the cart before the horse!

No one denies the need for nuclear deterrence—but it has to be matched by conventional deterrence. That has always been the ground reality. While nuclear deterrence is *subjective,* it is conventional deterrence that truly matters as it not only prevents a war but if the need arises, it ensures a credible response in our favour.

These have always been my views ever since I assumed concurrent charge as the chairman of the tri-service COSC. I had the opportunity to visit our forward areas along the Line of Actual Control (LAC) with China and it was then that I realised how paradoxical our situation was—*we were nuclear armed yet militarily fragile*.

MISPLACED PRIORITIES

We seem to be making the same strategic blunder as the Royal Navy of Britain in the 1960s and 1970s when it opted for the Polaris-Trident nuclear submarine programme.

That this was a national folly was realised much later by the atrophied British Royal Navy, when it could barely muster a motley group of ships to sail for the Falklands Operation in 1982. From a post-war Navy of unprecedented size, that boasted of more than 900 warships, including 52 aircraft carriers, it was stripped and emasculated within a span of barely 20 years and left with just two mothballed aircraft carriers in its inventory.

For us the message is clear. We may never need to fight a nuclear war but a conventional war can never be ruled out. Kargil nearly went that way.

And there will be many more Kargils and Dokhlams to deal with.

A LESSON FROM VAJPAYEE

It was in 1998, under Vajpayee's leadership, that India launched POKHRAN and joined the high table of nuclear-armed nations. Yet, the Prime Minister understood the importance of prudence where nuclear arms were concerned.

During the Kargil war, with defeat staring them in their faces, General Musharraf and his henchmen threatened nuclear retaliation but at the Cabinet Committee on Security, Prime Minister Vajpayee was unruffled by the rhetoric of the sabre-rattling Generals across the border and stood firm. Strategic restraint was his policy and such was his directive during the Kargil war to *evict the intruders, but without crossing the LOC.*

It reminded me of the didactic message in a poem written by Rudyard Kipling: *'If you can keep your head when all about you/ Are losing theirs.../If you can trust yourself when all men doubt you/But make allowance for their doubting too.../Yours is the Earth and everything that's in it...'*

CHAPTER 15

OFF THE CHEST: THE BARAK–TRISHUL CONTROVERSY

'Barak' is described in the Hebrew lexicon as a lightning strike. I will now narrate how a bolt from the blue struck me in the form of a bizarre controversy, which had been politically motivated.

•

Almost a decade after I had retired from the Indian Navy, it was on a relaxed autumn evening in October 2006 that I received a brief SMS from a close family friend: 'Watch the TV—something about George Fernandes and Sushil.'

I was stunned by what the electronic media was flashing as 'Breaking News—*Barak Controversy—Former Defence Minister George Fernandes and Ex-Navy Chief Sushil Kumar named in FIR*.'

After the initial shock had worn off, I got a sense of what it was all about. The so-called 'Barak controversy' of 2006, centred on an event that had taken place in June 1999 during the Kargil war, almost a decade back. It happened when I was the Navy Chief and George Fernandes was the Defence Minister.

DURING THE KARGIL WAR, 1999

Taking note of the Navy's war-fighting requirement, since full-scale hostilities seemed imminent, the Cabinet Committee on Security chaired by Prime Minister Vajpayee, approved the Navy's requirement for six Barak systems, which was the standard anti-missile defence (AMD) system for the Indian Navy and meant to augment the Barak systems already under procurement for INS *Viraat*, the Navy's aircraft carrier.

DRDO'S TRISHUL

During this cabinet meeting in June 1999, the boss of the Defence Research and Development Organization (DRDO) claimed he had a viable indigenous AMD system named Trishul. However, the government was aware of the true situation—that Trishul was a 'Top Secret' project, but had remained in limbo for fifteen years. It was for this reason that the cabinet ignored the spurious claims of the DRDO boss.

SKELETON IN THE CUPBOARD OF THE DRDO

It was this incident during the regime of George Fernandes

as Defence Minister that was being used by the rival political party in power to settle scores with a maverick politician who had always been a thorn in their flesh. Unfortunately, the Indian Navy and I, as the former Navy Chief, got dragged into this political crossfire.

The DRDO was given 10 years to produce Project Trishul (1982–92) and its mission was to develop an anti-missile defence (AMD) system for warships of the Indian Navy to counter the deadly sea-skimming missiles that Pakistan had secretly acquired from France. However, by 1990 it became apparent that the DRDO's AMD experiment was in the doldrums and by 1992, it was confirmed that its Project Trishul had failed. Since the Indian Navy had been left stranded, the government decided to immediately equip the Indian Navy warships with a suitable AMD system in lieu of the DRDO's defunct Trishul.

In 1992, a joint Navy–DRDO team of missile experts was thus constituted to comprehensively evaluate and recommend the best available option to replace DRDO's discarded Trishul system. Captain Sunil David was deputed by the Navy and Dr A.K. Kapoor, the project director for Trishul, was the DRDO's representative.

Technology for the AMD system at sea has always been a very closely guarded secret and in the mid-1990s only two countries were willing to part with such a system. After rigorous examination and conducting test trials abroad, the joint Navy–DRDO team recommended the Israeli Barak as the best option, since the only other system, the Russian Kaztan one, had miserably failed during the sea trials.

BARAK REPLACES TRISHUL, 1996

The Israeli Barak was thus approved by the government in 1996 as the AMD policy for the Indian Navy and remains so even today, with all Indian Navy frontline warships fitted with the Israeli Barak AMD system.

To avoid embarrassment to the DRDO, its abandoned Project Trishul was cloaked in a veil of secrecy and kept under wraps. But for the DRDO, the Israeli Barak's induction in the Indian Navy presented a new opportunity. Therefore, the DRDO quietly scuttled its own AMD experiments and signed up a joint venture with Israel to create Barak II for the future Indian Navy. And now the DRDO's Barak II has even got itself a Blue Ribbon tag as a 'Make in India' project.

MEDIA GOES TO TOWN

Blissfully unaware of the facts, the electronic media used the opportunity to garner TRPs with stories that suggested a collusion between the political leadership in 1999 and the Indian Navy. How did it matter that the armed forces were being maligned and brazenly politicised! Fake news, after all, can be more entertaining than boring facts!

The print media, unlike the TV channels, showed great maturity and methodically did its homework. After the noise and din of the electronic media had subsided, the newspaper headlines exposed the political skulduggery:

'Barak Backfires, Trishul Goes up In Smoke!'

THE TIMES

NAVY CHIEF SLAMS BARAK CASE AGAINST PREDECESSOR

FIR a 'matter of serious concern'

Navy Chief Reacts Strongly To Case Against Predecessor

TIMES NEWS NETWORK

New Delhi: The simmering unhappiness in Navy ranks over CBI's dragging its former chief, Admiral Sushil Kumar, into the Barak kickbacks case for allegedly pushing the Israeli anti-missile defence system over the indigenous Trishul AMD system burst out in the open on Monday.

Reacting to the CBI FIR against Kumar, Navy chief Admiral Arun Prakash said it was "a matter of serious concern". "We are trying to equip our armed forces for future conflicts, and if our equipment programme is going to be impeded in this manner, then it's a cause for concern. We must think seriously about it," he said.

Speaking to reporters on the margins of a conference, the Navy chief also forcefully rebutted the suggestion that Kumar had, at the behest of the then defence minister George Fernandes, promoted Barak's case even when the Israeli AMD had many flaws.

Admiral Arun Prakash

Giving the thumbs up to Barak-I, Admiral Prakash said: "The proof of the pudding lies in the eating. Out of 14 Barak tests, 12 have been direct hits. We have used them against low-flying surface-to-surface missiles."

The two unsuccessful tests, as reported by TOI earlier, were caused by "human error" and "a technical malfunction", not due to any overall systems failure. The claim that indigenous Trishul was passed over for Barak despite being a a better weapon system underpins CBI's case.

Admiral Prakash, however, was lavish in his praise of the Israeli system. "As far as we are concerned, the Barak system is very good. I don't think there is anything comparable today in any Navy," he said. Apart from Admiral Kumar, CBI has named George Fernandes, his party associates Jaya Jaitly and R K Jain, and alleged middle-man Suresh Nanda in its FIR in the Rs 1,160-crore Barak deal.

Admiral Prakash also dismissed claims that objections to the Barak-I deal from within the Navy were overlooked. The "dissent" by two senior officers was for the Barak-NG project between DRDO and Israel Aircraft Industries.

"In the Navy, everyone is allowed to give their frank opinion. But the final decision is taken by the chief after considering various inputs," said Admiral Prakash. His comment comes against the perception that CBI dragging Kumar in the case has not gone down well with the ranks.

104 ## 'POLITICISATION UPSETS MILITARY CHIEFS'

It was on 6 October 2006 that the Barak controversy was aired and the Chiefs of the three armed forces reacted strongly to the politicisation of the Indian armed forces, which dragged the Navy and its former Chief into a political squabble.

Admiral Arun Prakash, the serving Navy Chief and Chairman of the Chiefs of Staff Committee, spoke his mind and slammed the government in a public statement.

THE RTI ACT TO THE RESCUE

Though this entire episode was a farce, it was an agonizing time for me, since my lips had to remain sealed, the reason being that the matter was under the Official Secrets Act. I was also frustrated as my requests to meet the Defence Minister or the Prime Minister were completely ignored.

One day I happened to meet Josy Joseph, a talented defence analyst, who had worked with *Defence News and Analysis* and later *The Times of India*. He suggested that I consider the Right to Information Act to counter the Central Bureau of Investigation's (CBI's) bogus first information report (FIR) of 2006. I realised that it would be a dignified approach and decided to give it a try.

The central theme of the CBI's FIR was that Defence Minister George Fernandes and I, as Navy Chief, had not given due consideration to the DRDO's indigenous Trishul system. In reply, I sent an application to the Chief Information Commissioner, Wajahat Habibullah, with the brief preamble that Barak was the AMD system approved by the government in 1995 for the Indian Navy, as the DRDO's AMD experimental Project Trishul had failed.

As a result, this was the query that went to the MoD: Did the DRDO's Trishul AMD system ever exist?

For several weeks, the MoD stonewalled the query, claiming that it was too sensitive matter to be made public. Fortunately, every system has its checks and balances and the firmness and forthright manner in which the Central Information Commission handled the situation was truly praiseworthy. It gave the MoD a deadline of 14 days to explain.

Very conveniently, the MoD made the DRDO the scapegoat so the Commissioner made inquiries, asking the organisation to clarify what had actually happened. The DRDO sheepishly replied to the RTI query, admitting that: 'Trishul was a "Technology

Demonstrator" and after its assigned targets had been met, the project was wound up.' Knowing that Trishul never existed as an AMD system, the DRDO had given a devious explanation as an escape route for itself. The whole world knows that a 'Technology Demonstrator' is a euphemism for what is merely a 'Laboratory Experiment'.

The DRDO had not realised that its admission had incriminated its own erstwhile DRDO boss who falsely claimed during the Kargil war in 1999 that the DRDO's Trishul was a viable indigenous option fully developed by the DRDO as an AMD system. Thus it was that the DRDO's response to the RTI query created a serious crisis for the MoD.

THE AFTERMATH

The MoD realised it had committed a faux pas and quashed the CBI FIR of 2006 that had been filed four years ago. The Defence Minister's office then hurriedly contacted me, asking if I could meet Defence Minister A.K. Antony. I agreed and on 4th February 2010, I met A.K. Antony in the impressive South Block building, which houses the MoD and naval headquarters. I was on familiar ground and well prepared for this meeting.

From my body language, the Defence Minister must have sensed that I was aggrieved. So in the classical Pontius Pilate style, he washed his hands of his own responsibility and passed the buck to his predecessor.

I had come with a single-point agenda, which was to remind him that politicising the armed forces was unpardonable. And I did so, without mincing my words.

If you can keep your head when all about you are
losing theirs…
If you can talk with crowds… Or walk with Kings—
nor lose the common touch…

—Rudyard Kipling, circa 1895

PART III

THE VAJPAYEE LEGACY

President K.R. Narayanan and Prime Minister Atal Bihari Vajpayee being briefed by the author (right) at the Navy Day Reception in December 1999.

Prime Minister Vajpayee listening intently to Mrs Venita Kumar, wife of the author, at a Navy Day Reception.

THE VAJPAYEE LEGACY

It was at the turn of the new millennium that I was in command of the Indian Navy (1998–2001), appointed to serve as the Navy Chief when Atal Bihari Vajpayee was at the helm as the Prime Minister of India. It turned out to be the highlight of my military career but more than that it was an exhilarating experience that left a deep impression on me.

I had never met Prime Minister Vajpayee before my assignment as the Indian Navy Chief, nor did I have the opportunity to meet him after I retired from active duty but my experiences during those three years have crystallized into certain impressions of him as seen from a military perspective.

These impressions of mine are what I regard as the Vajpayee legacy and I do believe he has left behind a vital lesson for posterity, which would be of great value to leaders across the political spectrum—on how to handle the armed forces of the nation.

•

VAJPAYEE'S INSPIRATIONAL LEADERSHIP

The Kargil conflict erupted shortly after I took command of the Indian Navy and I have vivid recollections of those troubled times when it came to be realised that Pakistan's treacherous action on the Himalayan border had caught us unawares.

For Prime Minister Vajpayee, there must have been a sense of betrayal, as he had recently stretched out a hand of friendship with his historic bus trip to Lahore in Pakistan, inaugurating the bus service that connected Lahore and New Delhi. But he put all that behind him and looked ahead with a firm intent. His directive to the armed forces was unambiguous, instructing them to evict the intruders but not to cross the Line of Control (LoC).

The constraint of not crossing the LoC was undoubtedly a major tactical disadvantage for our frontline units who had the difficult task of evicting a well-entrenched enemy. But the Indian armed forces rose to the occasion and brought glory to the nation when they recaptured every bit of Indian Territory and drove out the Pakistani intruders.

It was with uncanny foresight that Prime Minister Vajpayee had imposed this severe tactical limitation on our frontline forces, for it finally turned out to be a masterstroke. With both adversaries being nuclear armed, the strategic restraint that Vajpayee exercised had instantly garnered international support and ensured that the war would be fought on India's terms. And what is also significant is that in this process, Vajpayee also called the bluff of General Pervez Musharraf and his Generals who had threatened nuclear retaliation.

HIS PERSONAL TOUCH

A characteristic feature of Prime Minister Vajpayee was his conscious effort to continually feel the pulse of his armed forces. As elaborated earlier in Chapter 1, it was within the first few days of the Kargil war that he instituted the procedure for the three Chiefs of the Army, Navy, and Air Force to meet him regularly at his residence for informal chats about our military ethos and frontline conditions. His was an earnest desire to understand our armed forces and what motivates them.

Not only did this personal interaction with him gain our confidence but it established an emotional bond with the rank and file of our armed forces. It was through his personal touch that Vajpayeeji infused synergy into our front line forces, which became evident during the Kargil war and several other operational events that followed.

HIS FINEST HOUR

Pakistan's treachery at Kargil was a personal setback for Vajpayeeji, but with an iron will and a positive approach, he rose to the occasion and galvanised the armed forces into action to combat the Pakistani intruders on the snow-covered Himalayan heights.

Reaching out to the rank and file of the armed forces, was the Vajpayee style of inspirational leadership and it was evident from the triumphant exertions of our front line forces, whose incredible feats of valour and sacrifice during Operation Vijay, resulted in hugely successful missions. He even met the Army troops in Kargil when the conflict was at its peak. It remains a lesson for posterity on how to motivate the nation's armed forces.

Two decades later while reconstructing the action sequences of the Kargil war, I find that Prime Minister Vajpayee's pivotal role during the conflict is blurred in the background, as if it has been lost in the fog of war. But that, I believe, is a reflection of his own modest and unassuming nature. He gave the entire credit to the armed forces, though undoubtedly it was his resilience and iron will that turned the tactical loss at Kargil into a strategic victory for the nation. That was his finest hour and that is how *faujis* of that era will always remember him.

●

VAJPAYEE'S TRANSFORMATIONAL APPROACH

In military terms it cannot be denied that Kargil caught us by surprise and this was the primary reason why Prime Minister Vajpayee constituted the Kargil Review Committee (KRC). His was a transformational approach, for he wanted to specifically address the lacunae within the system, as outlined earlier in Chapter 2.

With the acceptance of the KRC report, it became amply evident that the most important lesson that flowed out of Kargil was that the high-level command and control system was seriously flawed and inextricably linked to it was the vital need to operationally and logistically integrate the three armed forces with a well-defined military chain of command.

The Indian armed forces have for various reasons continued to function with the Chiefs of Staff Committee (COSC) system, which is a relic of the British Raj and completely out of sync with the requirements of modern warfare.

My experience as the Chairman of the COSC for almost two years is that apart from being an antiquated system, this committee has a vague operational charter. It is somewhat like a cooperative arrangement between the three service Chiefs whose basic priority remains their own respective parish. In short, it is just not structured to handle the strategic situation that we are confronted with today. Quite strangely, there are a few people within our military establishment and ill-informed outsiders as well, who still believe that there is nothing wrong with the existing COSC arrangement. Such resistance to change is nothing new and also existed in other major armed forces before their respective governments, such as in the US and the UK, took radical measures to revamp their armed forces and instal robust command and control structures.

It was with a transformational vision that Prime Minister Vajpayee had constituted the KRC which identified the systemic problems with great clarity. Many of the KRC recommendations, such as the Andaman and Nicobar Command and the Strategic Forces Command, are well in place today. However, the most important of them all, which was the recommendation to appoint a Chief of Defence Staff (CDS) to begin a system that would integrate theatre commands, could not be completed before Prime Minister Vajpayee's tenure ran out.

The critical need to restructure our armed forces with the CDS system has thus remained an operational imperative and one can only surmise that putting it in place in the future would require the Vajpayee type of transformational zeal.

●

VAJPAYEE THE SHEPHERD

An enduring impression that remains with me of my years with Prime Minister Vajpayee was the manner in which he kept his flock together and this was strikingly evident in the way he bridged the gap in the civil–military divide.

His painstaking efforts were directed towards inducing confidence within the system and creating an atmosphere of trust. The testimony to the success of his avowed mission was the mature relationship and understanding that existed between the government of the day and the armed forces. Viewed in hindsight, I do believe that Prime Minister Vajpayee's personal interaction with his three service Chiefs also had much to do with this.

Matching his 'good shepherd' approach was Prime Minister Vajpayee's remarkable political leadership and what impressed me was how effortlessly he managed a huge coalition government of disparate parties, with even the opposition parties invariably cooperating.

Brevity is the soul of wit and that, I realised, was Vajpayee's trademark. Being a man of few words, he never beat around the bush nor did he resort to jargon, always calling a spade a spade. The Prime Minister's unambiguous directive to the armed forces during the Kargil war remains a classic example of the Vajpayee touch.

The warmth he exuded in difficult situations had a soothing touch and this is best explained in the manner that he handled an extremely tricky operational situation that could have spiralled out of control with political and even international ramifications.

A STITCH IN TIME

Shortly after the Kargil war, with both sides in a high state of alert, an intruding Pakistani military aircraft was intercepted and shot down by Indian Air Force MIGs scrambled from the forward air base at Naliya in the Rann of Kutch. It was later learnt that the intruder belonged to an air squadron of Pakistan's Navy and was a French-built Breguet Atlantic aircraft that had a versatile capability for long-range maritime combat patrols at sea.

The Pakistani aircraft had left Mehran Naval Air Station shortly before 10 a.m. and the IAF ground radar tracked the plane as it approached the Indo-Pak border. The approach track of the aircraft was highly suspicious and the moment it crossed the border, the IAF sent the two MIGs for interception. There were a series of manoeuvres after the intruder entered Indian air space, during which the IAF pilots repeatedly advised the Pakistani aircraft to reverse course or land at a designated Indian air base. With absolutely no response forthcoming from the Pakistani aircraft, the IAF pilots were finally given clearance to shoot it down.

The intruder was brought down at 11.15 a.m., almost an hour after crossing the Indo-Pak border. What the intentions of the intruding Pakistani aircraft which stayed for an hour over Indian Territory were, has remained a mystery. For Pakistan's Navy, this was the only loss of an aircraft to hostile fire since the 1971 war.

By noon this information had reached Prime Minister Vajpayee who reacted with alacrity and directed that the Indian position needed to be urgently clarified to all political parties, well before the media got into the act. As Air Chief Marshal

Tipnis had already left for the forward air base at Naliya, Defence Minister George Fernandes directed me to conduct the briefing for the political dignitaries, which had been scheduled for that very same evening.

I realised that it was going to be a tough task, as it was entirely an Air Force matter—the only thing that concerned the Navy was that the intruding aircraft had belonged to Pakistan's Navy. Be that as it may, I was well briefed by our Air Force operations staff and was all set for a presentation, including video footage of the Pakistani aircraft wreckage that had been brought to Delhi's Palam airport. Present for this special briefing were senior cabinet ministers along with a galaxy of political luminaries from assorted coalition parties and senior members of the Opposition, which included Congress party's Mrs Sonia Gandhi and Manmohan Singh.

Frankly, I was quite nervous until Prime Minister Vajpayee took the stage. In his charismatic style, he thanked the dignitaries for attending the briefing at short notice and merely added that our armed forces remained ever vigilant as evident from the incident which happened just a few hours ago. I realised in a flash that Vajpayee's brief introduction had an instantly disarming effect and defused what could have been a tense situation.

The professional action of the Indian Air Force had obviously impressed the members present and thereafter the discussion was only about the Rann of Kutch, as the debris of the intruding Pakistani aircraft had been strewn across a vast swampy area there.

The presentation had been smooth sailing for me and I noticed that the members of the Opposition seemed particularly grateful that they had been taken into confidence by this thoughtful gesture of Prime Minister Vajpayee. This was indeed the typical Vajpayee touch.

•

VAJPAYEE'S STRATEGIC UNDERSTANDING

'Cometh the hour and cometh the man' has remained for centuries the accolade for a person who comes to the fore when the need arises. And I have always believed that after the initial setback at Kargil, Prime Minister Vajpayee came forth and transformed the situation by reversing the odds in India's favour. Apart from that, the decisive measures he took showcased his strategic understanding of the situation. As the Navy Chief, what impressed me most during the Kargil war was his understanding of the strategic role of a country's Navy. This became even more evident in later years when he brought in a refreshing new approach for dealing with China.

Prime Minister Vajpayee was deeply concerned that although the military equation between India and China had significantly altered since 1962 and both Asian giants were nuclear armed as well, the Peoples' Liberation Army's (PLA's) defiant intrusions across the Line of Actual Control (LAC) had forever kept us at a disadvantage.

But what greatly intrigued Vajpayeeji was the vastly different situation that prevailed at sea between the Chinese PLA Navy and the Indian Navy, as compared with the tense situation on the land border between the PLA and the Indian Army. While the two

Armies cautiously patrolled the LAC, there was always a healthy relationship and a professional understanding between the Navies.

This contrasting situation between the problematic land border and the normal atmosphere on the maritime front has never been understood by India's strategic planners. What was never appreciated was that this asymmetrical situation had a lot to do with the geographical and strategic advantage that India has in the Indian Ocean Region (IOR). Sitting astride China's energy lifeline which passes through the Indian Ocean has always given India the upper hand vis-à-vis China on the maritime front.

Prime Minister Vajpayee's understanding of what a Navy is all about had been triggered by what he had personally experienced during the Kargil war. Well before our Army and Air Force had swung into action, the Indian Navy had seized the initiative at sea. With the Indian Navy task forces sitting astride her energy lifeline which was her jugular, Pakistan's vulnerability lay exposed at sea.

This strategic manoeuvre of the Indian Navy had left a strong impression on Prime Minister Vajpayee and had a bearing on the approach that he subsequently adopted in dealing with China. It had become apparent to him that this was an asymmetrical situation in which India's operational advantage at sea had considerable potential for diplomatic leverage. Unlike the landward frontier with China, where we find ourselves tactically disadvantaged, the situation at sea is entirely in our favour.

With the Indian subcontinent positioned dominantly astride the Sea Lanes of Communication in the IOR, including China's new 'Silk Route', it is not India but China that finds itself on the back foot. The very thought of its energy lifeline being severed by the Indian Navy could be China's worst nightmare.

With his new-found understanding of the situation, Prime Minister Vajpayee realised that the time was opportune for a change of tack from the demeaning manner in which we had been kowtowing to China, with no answers to its defiant LAC provocations. Casting overboard the baggage of the past with its land-centric hangover and negative mindset, Prime Minister Vajpayee adopted a 'naval' approach, giving special emphasis to building the Indian Navy's strategic capability. In the years that followed, Prime Minister Vajpayee's foresight and wisdom became amply evident and the nation has much to thank him for it.

The induction of the powerful aircraft carrier battle group led by INS *Vikramaditya* has bolstered the Indian Navy's capability and completely transformed the strategic landscape of the IOR. In addition, the ICBM-firing nuclear submarine INS *Arihant* and other more potent SSBNs to follow provided the seaward leg of the nuclear deterrent with a second strike capability. The strident message that all this conveys is unlikely to be lost on China.

After his Kargil experience and aware of the professional understanding between the Chinese Navy and the Indian Navy, Prime Minister Vajpayee had given his personal approval for an extended deployment of an Eastern Fleet task force to the mid-China sea in the summer of 2000. It was meant to gauge the long-range capability of our Navy.

I recall this occasion quite vividly as the Ministry of External Affairs were rather concerned that this major naval deployment by India could send the wrong signal to the Chinese. However, on the contrary, after this extended sortie in the China Sea, which included joint exercises between the Chinese and Indian Navy units, a grand ceremonial reception was accorded by the Chinese to this Eastern Fleet task force when it entered Shanghai Port.

Well before our Indian Navy task force returned to its home base at Vishakapatnam, glowing reports from our Indian embassy in Beijing had arrived and it had been given wide coverage by not only China's television network, but the Western media, which had much to say about it as well. This came as no surprise to the Indian Navy but much more than that, it showcased Prime Minister Vajpayee's understanding of the Navy's strategic role and how it could be used to deal with China on equal terms.

For decades China had always exploited her tactical advantage along the LAC which has been an unresolved border since British colonial times. And the situation had been further compounded by China's claim that Arunachal was part of its middle kingdom. Prime Minister Vajpayee's approach in dealing with China had hinged on India's advantage on the maritime front. He used the diplomatic leverage it offered to offset the disadvantage that we have perpetually faced on the land border.

It is no coincidence that during the Vajpayee era, there was never a face-off with China of the type we had at Somdurong Chu in Arunachal in 1986 when India and China came close to a war or the major military confrontation at Dokhlam in 2017 with territorial claims by both China and Bhutan. As a Navyman, I remain convinced that this had much to do with Prime Minister Vajpayee's understanding of the strategic role of the Navy and the diplomatic leverage that can be brought to bear through maritime diplomacy or what has been known since Nelsonian times as 'gunboat diplomacy'.

●

VAJPAYEE'S CROWN OF THORNS

'Uneasy lies the head that wears a crown' wrote William Shakespeare and in a democracy the buck always stops with the Prime Minister who has to take the final call when a decision has to be made.

Apart from Kargil, there were other challenging operational situations that erupted during the Vajpayee era and I have vivid memories of those testing times, which added more thorns to Prime Minister Vajpayee's crown.

The attack by terrorists on 13 December 2001 targeting the Indian Parliament building in the heart of Delhi in broad daylight was one of the sharper thorns. Perpetrated by Pakistan army-sponsored terror groups, this audacious attack on the very citadel of Indian democracy shocked and infuriated the nation and the mood was for immediate retaliation.

The military Chiefs hurriedly met up with Defence Minister George Fernandes and NSA Brajesh Mishra at the Army operations room. I was then the chairman of the COSC, with Army Chief General Padmanabhan and Air Chief Tipnis as my colleagues. Our discussions were focused on delivering a swift riposte, which was the need of the hour and the contingency plan selected was to destroy a huge Pakistani Army training camp for terrorists located across the LOC and deep inside Pakistan Occupied Kashmir (POK). With our Army units in full readiness a last-minute intelligence report informed us that the camp had been cleverly relocated to a nearby site. However the site was located between a school and a huge hospital.

Frantic discussions took place and the final decision of the

Prime Minister was to stand down. Accordingly, this operation was aborted as striking the selected target would have resulted in unacceptable collateral damage.

With the option for a swift riposte having been shelved and the people still clamouring for immediate retaliation, the Cabinet Committee on Security (CCS) decided on full -scale mobilisation of the armed forces. The military Chiefs voiced their serious concerns since the purpose and aim of this mobilisation seemed unclear.

Codenamed Operation Parakram, the mobilisation may have been politically expedient but from a military point of view it led to massive dislocation of personnel and infrastructure with unjustified wastage of combat resources without any clear military aim or objective as no actual military action took place.

●

THE REQUEST BY THE US

As narrated earlier, it was after the 9/11 terror attacks in the US that a high-powered delegation arrived in India with a special request from the American President. The delegation unveiled the US plan to launch a global war on terror. Codenamed 'Enduring Freedom', the US operation had been planned to attack Afghanistan and decimate the Al Qaeda and Taliban.

What came as a surprise was that the US wanted major participation of the Indian armed forces in the US-led operation against Afghanistan and this turned out to be an extremely contentious issue at the CCS meeting that followed later in the day.

We three Chiefs vehemently opposed the idea of committing

the Indian armed forces for the US war against Afghanistan as this was not a UN mission and moreover, our armed forces were not part of any military alliance. On the other hand, the cabinet ministers were sharply divided on the issue. Once again, the Prime Minister showed his wisdom by not openly taking sides and quietly shelved the issue when he saw his military Chiefs were unanimously against it. All he said was that the matter needed some thought.

Quietly buried, the US proposal never saw the light of day.

•

A NEW DIMENSION TO TERROR

The hijacking of IC 814 brought in a new dimension to Pakistan's terror by proxy in which the Taliban based in Afghanistan was directly involved. It played out in the full glare of the electronic media and turned out to be a five-day ordeal for the entire nation.

As the three military Chiefs were required to attend the CCS meetings, it gave us a ringside experience. Those were perhaps the most stressful days for Prime Minister Vajpayee and his cabinet ministers.

Swapping five notorious Pakistani terrorists held in Indian jails for an entire plane load of Indian passengers was the non-negotiable demand of the Taliban hijackers and their ruthless intentions had been clearly demonstrated when they stabbed one passenger to death and brutally injured 17 others.

31 December 1999 was the deadline for the ultimatum and with the hijacked plane under Taliban control in Kandahar, the

Indian government found itself devoid of options. Not only did we lack the wherewithal for a long-range Israeli-style Entebbe operation, but the only opportunity that presented itself when the plane touched down at Amritsar for refuelling, was lost through inaction by the Crisis Management Group in New Delhi.

With the Taliban ultimatum fast approaching, the CCS had to take a decision. Submitting to the hijackers' demand went squarely against the grain but the lives of so many Indian citizens was at stake and this was the dilemma that faced Prime Minister Vajpayee.

With the cabinet sharply divided and the relatives of the passengers clamouring at his door, all eyes were on the Prime Minister on the final day of the Taliban ultimatum. He and only he had to make the decision. And as the nation waited with bated breath, Vajpayeeji gave his nod for the swap to be done.

As I reflect on that solemn moment, I wonder what may have gone on in the mind of the Prime Minister. He knew that giving into the demand of the hijackers was patently wrong and could perhaps lead to serious consequences. Yet at the same time to have the blood of innocent Indian citizens on his hands was not something that anyone could live with. This five-day ordeal would surely have been a proverbial bed of nails for Prime Minister Vajpayee.

One can only conjecture on what the consequences would have been had Prime Minister Vajpayee's decision been otherwise. But I do believe that given the situation that prevailed in real time, any other Prime Minister in Vajpayee's place could not have done it differently.

●

VAJPAYEE'S APPROACH TO TERRORISM

The Kargil conflict was an inflection point in Prime Minister Vajpayee's approach to terrorism which was being directed at India from Pakistani soil. There were different strands of 'terrorism by proxy' that were inflicted on India, as evident from General Musharraf's Himalayan folly in 1999, followed by the hijacking of IC 814 to Kandahar and finally, the brazen attack on our Parliament in December 2001. But the common thread that linked these terrorist actions was the nefarious hand of Pakistan's Army and its Inter-Services Intelligence (ISI) agency, whose notoriety goes back to the cold war era.

The Pakistani military junta dubbed as the 'Deep State' were always aware of their own limitations compared to India's military might and growing international stature. It therefore resorted to the thoughtless and reckless measure of colluding with home-grown terror outfits for its campaign of 'terror by proxy'. This remains till today the trademark of the Pakistani Army's sinister design of waging a sub conventional war that would bleed India with its hydra-headed terrorist proxies. Moreover, it provides the Pakistani 'Deep State' a convenient tool of deniability to demonstrate its 'good boy' image.

In the political conscience of Pakistan, there may be an abiding desire to wrest control of Kashmir. But the ground reality is that Pakistan's Army unequivocally calls the shots and its singular aim is to avenge the humiliating defeat by the Indian armed forces in the 1971 Indo-Pak war.

Prime Minister Vajpayee had clearly understood Pakistan's intentions of needling India and its modus operandi of using terror outfits as its proxies. However, he also had no illusions about the limitations of our own military capability, which had to deal with the strategic nexus between Pakistan and China. India could ill afford to lower its guard along the 4050-kilometre LAC on the Chinese front.

Prime Minister Vajpayee's resilience and foresight had carried the day during the Kargil war but the hijacking of IC 814 and the brazen attack on our Parliament turned out to be a different story. Our options were heavily constrained by inadequate military wherewithal.

In 1999, when the IC 814 hijacking took place, we lacked the capability to carry out a long-range Entebbe type of raid, Israeli style. Accordingly, the Vajpayee government had been left with no options when negotiations reached an impasse and inevitably, succumbed to the demands of the Taliban hijackers.

In the aftermath of the attack on the Parliament in December 2001, public anger and hysteria clamoured for immediate retaliation against Pakistan. Unfortunately, the contingency operation that was in readiness to attack a terrorist camp deep inside POK had to be aborted due to the unacceptable collateral damage that could have resulted. After intense discussions, Prime Minister Vajpayee directed the armed forces to stand down on the operation. Soon thereafter the CCS went into damage control mode and hastily ordered the mobilisation of the armed forces. Deeply perturbed, we military Chiefs voiced our concern, as there seemed to be no clear aim or strategic objective that could explain the rationale for full-scale mobilisation of the three armed forces. It was certainly not for war and Prime Minister Vajpayee knew that too.

Operation Parakram, as it came to be known, could at best serve as a means for coercive diplomacy. In essence, it was sheer political expediency that had prompted the decision. Arguably, coercive diplomacy can be an effective measure provided it is carefully calibrated with a clear-cut strategic aim. More importantly, it has to be matched alongside with a robust military capability. But this was not so and added to our woes. The purpose of Operation Parakram has thus remained an unresolved debate even to this day.

Seen in hindsight, there is a lesson to be learnt for addressing the persistent problem of Pakistan's terrorism by proxy. Quite clearly, we are living in a dangerous neighbourhood and if we hope to deter Pakistani terrorism, we must not forget the age-old maxim: Prosperity and security are two sides of the same coin.

India is today regarded as an ascending power with strong democratic credentials, while Pakistan on the other hand is on a slippery slope as a global sponsor of terror. In addition to that, it would be prudent to factor in the inexplicable nexus between Pakistan and China whose converging aim is evidently to undermine India's growth and international stature. To believe that Pakistan will readily change its ways under growing international pressure is wishful thinking. That could only happen when Pakistan's Army no longer calls the shots, which itself is just a pipe dream.

The nation has to brace itself for the long haul to deal with the pernicious designs of the Pakistani 'Deep State' and to counter its campaign of 'terror by proxy' would require robust measures for 'homeland security' alongside a potent military capability. What is also clear is that the challenge posed by global terrorism today requires a different security framework in which the Indian armed forces should play the lead role. They are the nation's front line force and best equipped to do so.

Being essentially configured for a wartime role may require the three armed forces to realign their technological sights for a dual mission of a 'full-scale war' and 'counter-terrorism' on the home turf. The experiences of countries such as the US are well documented so we do not need to look too far for ideas. However, what would be prudent for our policymakers would be to invest in our nation's security by revamping our military capability. That is the most critical need of the hour.

●

WHAT WE COULD LEARN FROM VAJPAYEE

The Indian armed forces are graded as the world's largest *volunteer* force but they are also considered to be one of the most disciplined military establishments with an unparalleled track record of sacrifice and dedication to the nation.

The apolitical ethos of the Indian armed forces stems from their oath of allegiance wherein *the safety, honour, and welfare of the country come first—always and every time.* But it is not just their apolitical ethos nor is it their martial ardour or ceremonial grandeur but their legendary sacrifice and dedication to the nation in war and peace that makes them a robust pillar of our society and endears them to the citizens of the country.

Prime Minister Vajpayee's conscious effort was to get to know and understand the distinctive features of Indian military ethos and with his personal rapport motivated and inspired our frontline forces.

Seen in the context of national security, Prime Minister Vajpayee's handling of our armed forces as an instrument of state policy, was quite unique and the lesson it offers would be of great value to politicians and leaders. In essence, his was a pragmatic approach that addressed the sad truth reflected in poetic verse by Rudyard Kipling:

In times of war and not before,
God and the soldier are adored
But in time of peace and all things righted,
God is forgotten and the soldier slighted.

CHANGE OF GUARD: Chief of Army Staff Gen S. Padmanabhan with the author after taking over the baton of Chairman of the Chiefs of Staff Committee (COSC) on 31 December 2001.

The author with his wife Venita Kumar after assuming charge of the Indian Navy in December 1998. Also seen is the Admiral's Flag Lieutenant (ADC).

Top to bottom:

- The author greets former Prime Minister I.K. Gujral at a Navy Day Reception.
- The author with L.K. Advani who was the Deputy Prime Minister in the Vajpayee Cabinet.
- External Affairs Minister Jaswant Singh and the author shared a common interest in equestrian sport.

Top to bottom:

• The author and his wife Venita Kumar exchange pleasantries with Congress president Sonia Gandhi at a Navy Day Reception.

• National Security Adviser Brajesh Mishra arrives for a Navy Day Reception.

• The author and his wife Venita Kumar bid farewell to First Lady Usha Narayanan at the Rashtrapati Bhavan, New Delhi in December 2001.

EPILOGUE

It was early 1998 when I was stationed at Kochi, playing out the final innings of my naval career as the Commander-in-Chief of the Southern Naval Command.

With just about a year left for retirement from active duty, my wife Venita and I had commenced planning on how we would shift from the mainland to our retirement home at Port Blair, in the far-off Andaman Islands. We had decided to spend our final years by the seaside, with our menagerie of pet dogs, cats, rabbits and geese—known in Navy parlance as 'Swallowing the anchor'.

Then suddenly, it all changed.

By an Act of Parliament, the retirement age for all Central government employees was extended by two years, which meant that I had almost three years of active service still remaining.

Apart from all plans for retirement being shelved, I found myself fortuitously placed on top of the heap as the most senior serving Commander-in-Chief because all my batchmates and contemporaries, who were older than me, had since retired from active duty. Shortly thereafter, being the most senior Vice Admiral in the Navy, I was duly promoted to the rank of a four-star Admiral on 30 December 1998 and appointed in command of the Indian Navy.

That is how I happened to serve as an armed forces' Chief during the tenure of Atal Bihari Vajpayee as the Prime Minister of India.

WHY IS VAJPAYEE REMEMBERED TODAY?

As the world's largest democracy, India can boast of several great statesmen who have been at its helm. But what makes Prime Minister Atal Bihari Vajpayee stand out was his inimitable political leadership that struck a chord across the political spectrum. That is why Vajpayee is being fondly remembered even today, decades later.

Managing a coalition government comprising disparate political parties can be a bed of nails, but what impressed me during the Vajpayee era was the cohesive style of the Prime Minister. He kept his flock together with a charismatic touch that even motivated the Opposition parties to remain in synchronisation.

Added to this was the Prime Minister's pragmatic approach in addressing the chronic problem of civil–military relations. This turned out to be greatly beneficial for the military, as it ensured a mature relationship and understanding between his government and the armed forces.

FAREWELL TO ARMS

I retired from active duty on 30 December 2001 and I vividly recall the final moments during my formal call on the Prime

Minister at his residence. The three years I had served with him flashed through my mind as I met him for the last time, to bid farewell.

Those were eventful years with several challenging situations, ranging from the Kargil war of 1999 to the terror attack on our Parliament in 2001. Prime Minister Vajpayee had been very closely involved with the military and this motivated officers as well as the rank and file, bringing out the best in them when dealing with these situations.

The rapport that Prime Minister Vajpayee maintained with our armed forces stemmed from his desire to understand the Indian military ethos with its apolitical character and secular fabric. This has remained the Vajpayee legacy and this is how the military will always remember him.